MANAGING SCHOOLS

John Sayer

(*Advisory editor*: Professor Denis Lawton)

Hodder & Stoughton
LONDON SYDNEY AUCKLAND TORONTO

349057

British Library Cataloguing in Publication Data
Sayer, John, *1931—*
  Managing schools. — (Studies in teaching and
  learning) 1. Great Britain. Schools. Management
  I. Title II. Lawton, Denis, *1931–* III. Series
  371.2'00941

ISBN 0 340 41670 X

First published 1989

Phototypeset by Input Typesetting Ltd, London
Printed in Great Britain for the educational publishing division of
Hodder and Stoughton Limited, Mill Road, Dunton Green,
Sevenoaks, Kent by Page Bros (Norwich) Ltd

Contents

1 Introduction   1

2 Values and Management   15

3 Change and Arrest   29

4 Managing the Community Dimension   45

5 Management and Teachers   66

6 School Financial Responsibility   85

7 Developing the Heart of Schools   105

Appendix: The Proposed General Teaching
          Council   119

Bibliography   126

Index   129

ONE

Introduction

Why this book?

This book is about managing schools. It does not start from the study of concepts of school management, although that may well emerge from looking at improvements of practice. Rather it addresses the issues of managing schools for all: of a society's participation in the way schools are run and where they are going. These issues transcend current ventures, and offer a context by which they may be judged.

In every round of teachers' conferences and political elections, we are told that schools are in crisis. That is what attracts media coverage, and is also a pre-condition in a market economy for high-profile attention-seeking political interventions. There appear to be two extremes of cure-all prescription: to keep hands (usually other people's hands) off the schools, or radical change from central government to spell out precisely what schools should do and make sure they do it. There are hidden and overt agendas. Somewhere between the extremes is a less than responsible mood of kaleidoscope management. If you are tired of the pattern, give it a shake and take credit for whatever new pattern emerges, whether through market forces or through the concern of parents and teachers to make anything work for children.

Good management is either to enable schools to look after themselves, or to ensure that they do as they are told. 'We have the direction, now we want the director' was the catch-phrase of one recent advertisement. Not surprisingly, it did not catch. Management is itself a part of controversy and dispute. A school or service which gets on with the job without support or intervention is not the best instrument of interventionist educational or political policies, and may be frowned upon; a school which goes by the book is likely to be lifeless. There is no such thing as good management in itself. What is meant by good management depends on what we want schools to

1

be and to do. Management is not a free-standing discipline; it is a hybrid of intentions and skills, an application of basic disciplines brought together in the common purpose which justifies and prompts them all; the improvement (however conceived) of the species and its environment.

So a book about school management has to start with some view of what we want for humanity and its contexts of physical environment and inherited learning. It has to be about education first, and a particular instrument of schooling only second. In previous eras the two have been closer than they are today. The notion of a school is not now so close to fundamental thinking about education as it appears to have been in some previous periods. School also no longer encompasses the major channels of learning. It does not have its former supreme importance. There are other media, better for some purposes, more accessible and less unwieldy than school systems. The real crisis in schools is not the headline stuff at all: it is more to do with whether schools are the right tool for learning at all, and if so, what forms of learning.

The next decade will be one of sharply pointed political blandishments. There will be erratic power lusts to satisfy at the expense of energy which has to be devoted to finding common cause; there will be power struggles nationally, regionally, and locally, many of them related to single issue politics and trying to relate the governance of schools to single issues. The relationship of school and community will not be one of sweet fudge. I am assuming, notwithstanding all this, that schools will be about learning experience involving whole local communities in sharing responsibility for future generations; and that national or supra-national direction of school systems, given time, will be about encouraging that local sharing process. A further assumption is that by promoting positive contributions to and from all parts of the local community, the medium of school education will be enabled to adjust continuously to the context of other forms of learning available to that community, whether from its own resources or from distance media. These assumptions will only become reality if people are organised to bring them about. I shall be supposing, moreover, a common will towards making sense of resources at present fragmented by age boundaries and notional differences of activity. In most countries there will be a shift in focus towards a third age extended by lower ages of retirement and longer spans of life, together with a medley of life and work styles from age eighteen into the forties, with less stable employment adding to part-involvement of adults both in the learning and running of schools and colleges.

School, if it is to have a future meaning, will be an orchestration of instruments previously atuned to solo performance: nursery, infants, junior and secondary schools, local colleges, youth and adult education, institutional and non-institutional services, formal and informal, general and vocational, full and part-time. It is because of current divisions of habit, perception and system, that immediate political programmes are imposing even greater fragmentation without rhyme or reason, and that organised single-issue pressure groups are gaining control of government and public audiences. A quest for coherence and longer-term aims is in a much fuller sense political.

Locally, too, a variety of defence mechanisms and power struggles should be expected; but if they are anticipated they can be more readily accommodated. People in schools are too puritanical about power, not least about their own, which is considerable. Shared local governance of schools will either be about accountability to complaining customers able to opt elsewhere; or it will be about the bonds of school and community in shared responsibility for learning and future life chances. If teachers opt out of power or try to retain it, the market-force model will emerge; if the choice is one of shared commitment and responsibility not just for outcomes but for decision making and process, schools will continue to have a part in the education of all.

From such assumptions as these, there are sets of consequences for the way schools are run. One is that they are no longer going to be organised as though they were complete in themselves. Another is that their organisation and its members will be facing outwards to meet other outward-facing organisations, groups and individuals. A third is that those who work from a school base will do so with a professionality trained to be explicitly open and cooperative. A fourth is that such open sharing and cooperative modes of management will be part and parcel of the school learning experience.

That makes sense only as a preparation for social reconstruction, however unfashionable in the national rhetoric. Already, I have been making an assumption without prior justification that other groups in a local community – related professions, voluntary associations, bases of employment, families, pubs and clubs, local councils – will also be committed to facing outwards, sharing insights and resources, making sense together, and being part of a common and continuing commitment to learning. That requires a revolution in all those other bases of employment and activity, not just in schools. School democracy does not mean giving power to a locality's perpetuated hierarchies and squirarchies or to minority activist demagogues. It can only make sense as part of social adjustment as a whole; the school service may need to take the first steps; but the direction has to be agreed by those who will have to accompany or follow.

This book is intended, therefore, not only for those in the education service who are at present managing schools or thinking of doing so. It is not only for those beyond the trained teaching profession who have a caring involvement in the way schools are run or what they bare to offer in the future. It is setting down markers for management in industry and commerce, and in local community services. In the last decade or two, the education service has been borrowing management notions from other employment sectors; in the next decade or two, it will have the task of redemption, not only of mortgage loans. Education is a vast employment sector engaging over half a million professional teachers, hundreds of thousands of other employees, and at least ten million direct clients in Britain alone; as such, it has the duty, as do other major centres of activity, to prompt and promote good practice elsewhere. Recent research, against the current assumptions, has indicated that on the whole schools are better managed than 'industry'. So whilst the Department of Trade and Industry sets its sights on teachers using their holidays to learn about good management from industry, we should be looking for some reciprocal benefits. Even more, the organised education service is also society's projection of its own future intent, and that applies to the way it manages its business affairs. Education management has to be about democracy meaning business, not just in schools. It has to be addressed outwards. Most of the current literature is addressed inwards, even if the content may also be about looking outwards. To leave it there would be bad management.

Future issues

Teaching and managing

It is by now the conventional wisdom that school leaders are both leading professionals and chief executives (Hughes, 1973). This is a distinction which I have found more and more difficult to retain, and which will be queried in this book. It derives both from theories of organisation and from the politics of acceptability in schools.

A particularly valuable recent volume in this series reminds us that all organisations have essentially three interrelated components: people, structures, and resources (Hoyle, 1986). Eric Hoyle follows earlier exponents in dwelling on the people and structures, reminds us of the middle ground of people in groups but, using the hourglass image, observes that school systems have a somewhat thin connection between the organisation and the direct teaching-learning process: 'At the present time, there is little to suggest that there is a systematic relationship between the managerial domain and the core task dimension of teaching and learning' (Hoyle, 1986). Now management is about that interrelatedness. Hoyle does acknowledge positive signs in those studies which marry process and climate in a concept of effectiveness. I hope to show that the related element of resource management is also a strong connector: resource as a concept and approach, of which 'resources', schools and teachers are all a part, as are learning skills. Managing resources, therefore, figures more prominently here than in most general volumes, but not as a matter of nuts and bolts.

Many have made the distinction between professional (teaching) and management roles in a school, and have emphasised the need for balance between them. Perhaps this has been a justification for having as managing director of a school a person appointed as head-teacher. It may also be offered as a justification for insisting that there are dimensions of headship which are different from those of teaching and learning, and which may require training. This is understandable, given the background both of organisational theory and of learning theory against which ideas have developed, and the training mission of those who have developed them. I believe, how-ever, that this approach can be transformed through the pursuit of resource and skill. This leads me to the view not that schools should be run by managers as distinct from teachers, but that all teaching is about management and that much which is projected as 'manage-ment' is a form of learning valuable for all. So I shall be seeking to articulate a continuum of management within and beyond the school. That brings with it a particular approach to leadership styles and qualities; if there is to be a 'covenant of leadership' (John, 1980) it will not be confined to heads and the latest jargon of senior manage-ment teams; nor will it be entirely internal to the professional organis-ation of schools.

School organisations

This is a book about the issues and responses facing schools in the forseeable future. It is grounded in practice. That does not divorce it from studies of organisational theory. On the contrary: most theory is developed when and because it is needed in practical problem solving; applicable concepts are generalised from practical situations.

Studies of schools as organisations have started from the premise, which should not be left unquestioned, that schools *are* organisations. Schools have been examined as either 'tight' or loosely structured organisations. Societies go through phases in which they would wish schools to be more or less tightly structured. At moments of insecur-ity, a society will want to 'do something' about its schools, to secure the future, and anachronistically will tend to blame present schooling for the inadequacies which have led to perceived political, economic or moral decline from earlier standing or standards. This appears to be the prevalent mood in Britain. General optimism for the future, on the other hand, and the belief in a future which will not repeat the mistakes of the past, appears to unleash the system, to encourage development, and not to burden schools with too much received wisdom. This was more the mood of post-war social reconstruction, however unevenly or inadequately applied. It was reflected in the very name of the Schools Council for Curriculum and Examinations, just as the abolition of the Schools Council and the seizure of curriculum and examinations by national government has reflected the social insecurity of the last decade. Whether or not a school has responsibility for what it is doing will have some bearing on whether it is an organisation to manage in any full sense, and what will be the nature of the organisation, the ethos and the style of management.

Organisations are circumscribed by boundaries, however permeable. It is not easy to agree whether schools are organisations at all. If they are not, that is a problem for organisation theory; if they are or if it is supposed that they should be, then schools can be usefully considered alongside non-school organisations. I am not arguing here the case for a phenomenological approach, in which the organisation exists only as far as it exists in the consciousness of individual actors or audience. Rather, I am questioning the notion of the school. In what sense, for example, is a primary school of ten teachers an organisation, whilst the faculty of a secondary school or the department of a technical college is not? In what sense is the primary head more a manager than the secondary head of faculty? In what sense is a small school more or less the branch of a local authority than is the faculty or department of a large school or college? Is the boundary between two similar primary schools more or less defined within an education service than is the boundary between two different faculties or administrative divisions in a secondary school? Is the boundary between two similar faculties in different secondary schools more or less defined than either of the previous examples? Some of us have been involved in federal schools, with some form of *Dachorganisation* or umbrella organisation across the different parts. Is the University of London an organisation with its constituent colleges as sub-structures, or are the colleges the organisations, with the university as a form of association? Whatever may be the perception there, it will not be the same as the collegiate structure of Oxford, for example, with its larger number of much smaller colleges, or of the University of Wales with its greater distances.

Constitutional law may give us one set of answers relating to legal responsibility; but these are peripheral to management. There are a growing number of loose school amalgamations: 'clusters', some for all purpose, some for one purpose only. There are units or centres, on or off site, which are neither schools in a legal sense nor part of the school organisation. How shall we handle the next stage of distance learning from open university through open college to open school? These variants will increase as an education service seeks to become more flexible in response to local community needs and new means of access. It will be more difficult to describe education in terms of a school.

However we may answer such questions it is becoming clearer in current practice that schools are not *isolated* organisations, however much current legislation may seek to isolate them. Corporate management across organisations and services is increasingly important and engages increasing proportions of time and concern. Five years ago, surveys among heads of schools were showing external management as low on the league tables of preference, perceived importance and training need (Jones, 1987); by now, whatever the preferences, all heads recognise the importance and the need to develop skills in managing outwards, in boundary management, in networks.

The range is enormous, even across professional services, from planning the contribution each school or service may make to a community, through to the contribution each of the various services may make to a child in need. Once we adopt the notion of a contributory society, in which individual and corporate skills and supplies are to be shared and 'vired' to agreed priority use, what matters most is an organisation which covers the interstices and which communicates across centres. So it may be the communication across schools and between schools as a group and other contributory services, which emerges as the educative organisation of the future, with schools as substations, rather as departments are now seen as substructures in the school organisation. A helpful parallel is of libraries which can now be linked in an inter-library network. There are parallels, too, among the more parasitic trades and professions: wholesalers, travel agencies and banks. In schools, the current notion of choice through open enrolment has to be turned into access to all resources from whatever point of the system, from naked competition to open cooperation.

New technologies

Such shifts in priority are all part and parcel of a revolution of communications and information technology, which will shortly have affected radically both the background administration and the direct learning processes which have been associated with schools, and which will have made it possible to merge direct and indirect modes of learning. Access to information of all kinds is already largely through channels other than schools, and is not controlled by schools or the education service. So the school curriculum in the formal sense is not so important in itself as it was even twenty years ago. Politicians who now concern themselves with a national curriculum for schools are that much out of date, whatever the arguments for or against central control or uniformity. There is no future in trying to put the whole of a broad and balanced curricular experience into the school framework, without reference to the variety of learning opportunities or lack of them beyond school. The future must be with coordination across learning resources. So inter-organisational cooperation becomes the core organisation.

Managing learning

The dimension of managing resources will also be strongly related to the learning experience of groups: people as a resource to each other's learning, 'maieutics', 'synergy;' particular individual skills brought to contribute to cooperative learning; and individual learning assisted by teams. There is a strong social psychology component here, bridging across ground disciplines, as indeed does management. Part of our society continues to talk of the 'good school,' with assumptions and overtones of elitism; part of the professional language, on both sides of the Atlantic, has in the last decade been about the 'effective' school. There are some objections to the notion of effectiveness, but at least it offers a set of codes through which to communicate between those who determine resources and those who are teaching. Indeed, that gap is now bridged, with the teacher as an organiser of learning experiences and therefore of the resources for learning, self included. The real issue is not whether the teaching profession should be able to manage resources; it is whether the value systems which determine what is learned and how it is learned are ends or means: whether they are the purpose for which money is raised, or whether money-raising is the main purpose of learning. For most young people going through the latter years of schooling, the aims of education as declared in a school prospectus are acceptable only as a means or an accompaniment to getting a job. The fact that most in the foreseeable future will not get a job as a direct outcome of compulsory schooling will either cause increasing school rejection or it will cause parents, young people and their teachers to re-think what are the purposes of learning and why it is worth paying for, from their time and from the public purse.

As just one example of the proximity of direct learning processes and skills of management, we might consider an extract from a current leaflet:

   (a) formula ideas/problems:
      (i)   *identify*, understand and describe the task;
      (ii) label elements correctly, identify *concepts*;
      (iii) gather and record necessary *information* correctly;
      (iv) *choose* appropriate 'tools';
      (v) employ appropriate system or *reference* and use it effectively.
   (b) planning strategies:
      (i)   *define* the objectives;
      (ii) seek a *strategy* for tackling the task;
      (iii) recognise *alternatives*;

(iv) *organise* the work effectively;
(v) *adapt* the chosen strategy.
(c) evaluating ideas/evidence:
    (i) identify different *points of view*;
    (ii) *discriminate* . . . what is relevant;
    (iii) *interpret* evidence;
    (iv) discriminate in tests of *value*.
(d) use ideas, procedures and 'tools':
    (i) follow *instructions*;
    (ii) use *procedures*;
    (iii) *adapt* procedures to contexts;
    (iv) *apply* ideas to different contexts;
    (v) use tools with effective *technique*.
(e) *make* and justify judgments:
    (i) make sound *judgments*;
    (ii) *explain* judgments clearly;
    (iii) *justify* decisions made;
    (iv) *check* the product carefully;
    (v) *modify* judgments in the light of new evidence.

This could be the outline of a systematic approach in a course of management training. Instead, it is in fact a checklist for assessing children's cognitive skills, prompted by the requirements of GCSE coursework, though not confined to that age group (Oxfordshire Skills Programme, 1987). There has long been a recognisable proximity between skills of management, as developed in training programmes, and basic learning skills as developed in the processes of primary schooling. What is relatively new is the bridge across secondary and further education, through the conceptualisation of a skills-based curriculum and through the rediscovered emphasis on process.

The change is partly in response to recently identified learning needs, partly the recognition that the store of knowledge is accumulating and changing so rapidly that shared access and skills of retrieval are more appropriate than capacity to store in the memory of any one individual. That recognition brings about changes not just in the learning process, but in the enabling organisation. Teachers are not there to teach , but to open access both by unlocking resources and by unlocking resourcefulness. The way they and other resources are deployed has to be adapted to their different role, otherwise they cannot be effective. We can no longer afford to have a gap between the processes of the organisation and the learning processes it is there to promote.

The hidden curriculum

The organisation is itself a strong part of the learning environment and the learning experience. It may be described as 'hidden curriculum', though its messages are glaringly obvious. The style of manage-

9

ment, in particular, is going to be part of all young people's learning experience and their perceptions of society's future intentions. So a tightly circumscribed or strongly hierarchical style will reduce the credibility of an open-ended or participative approach to a negotiated curriculum. A teacher cannot liberate whilst bearing chains. The same consistency is required in reverse: teachers who are liberated and participate freely in corporate decisions must make sense of their own freedom by promoting it in the way others are able to take responsibility for their learning; or else all we have achieved is a transfer from autocracy to oligarchy, from monarchy to petty princedom which is all the more damaging for being more direct. We shall have to explore the effects of a 'senior management team' not just on the rest of a professional group but on young people and their families.

Alongside the family, a school is the main instrument by which adult society signals and should enact to the next generation its intended relationships, value systems and priorities. Our society as a whole appears to have endorsed the principle of equal opportunities. It should be possible to promote the practice of equal opportunity in the way schools are organised. Teaching is one of the few professions in which there are a majority of women. This is not reflected in the management structures of schools, and even less in further education or administration. Equal opportunities legislation had the immediate and unintended effect of *reducing* women's access to senior management teams in schools, following the ruling against statutory positions for a senior master or mistress of the other sex. There are parts of the country where it is virtually unknown for a woman to be head of a mixed comprehensive school. Over the last twenty years, the number of women appointed to be chief education officer of a local authority has ranged from nil to a mere handful. These are just the most obvious manifestations. The positive action required is not so much to give preference to women as to combat prejudice among governors, teachers and parents, very often amongst women themselves, against having women in positions of leadership. It is confidence that needs promoting. That has to be part of a school's planned policy, with targets.

The issues of race and colour are similar, but more complex. There are particular problems of mismatch in local contexts, which require solutions some of which lie beyond the locality, for example in access to the national patterns of initial teacher-training. There are proliferated issues of language, culture and faith. Again, one of the most powerful instruments of social reform is a visible policy to work in schools towards a professional group and governing body which reflect what we want a community to become.

Such signals for the future will include the school's employment and career development of the handicapped. They will include a professional struggle, very little in evidence to date but about to be imposed at least within the European Communities, to secure international mobility of the profession as part of a witness to international outlooks and understanding. There will be controversial issues, related to patterns of behaviour, political outlook, regional provenance and dialect. These may or may not be worked out in a local education authority; what shows for young people is how they are resolved in a school.

The context of change

The context of schools is not just one of frequent changes, but of constant change. Change is now the one stable element on which to establish a system of education. Erratic movement is caused by obstacles to change rather than by the flow of change itself. The management of change is no longer about innovating single major reforms; it is about a process of constant review, revision, realignment, renewal and reform. Neither the seventeenth- to eighteenth-century view of progress as the growth of the tree of human knowledge, nor the Hegelian or Marxist perspectives of progress through necessary conflict are adequate. What does an institution look like if, despite the very root of its meaning, it is not static? The question is addressed not just to those schools which recognise and plan for change, but to those which appear not to change with the times. Some of the most drastic changes, usually for the worse, are brought about by schools and services standing still and changing nothing whilst the context of public and personal needs is changing. Occasionally, this may be a deliberate strategy; if so, it is part of a planned change of relationship with the context, something like walking on the spot on an escalator. How can we envisage a 'disestablishment?' That must be the leading question and therefore the first part of this book.

New legislation

The question becomes the more intricate as those other long-standing institutions of parliamentary democracy and legislation attempt sporadically to control and direct the school process and structure. Major enactments related to education have previously been some decades apart; between them, there have been generations of schooling. To reach the statute books they have, moreover, taken two or three decades after committees or major shifts in thinking have prompted proposals for change. National laws are now being laid down as a prelude to desired change rather than as a delayed acceptance of what has been happening already or a recognition of the general will. The 1980, 1981, 1985 (further education), 1986, 1987 and 1988 education acts will all have contained ingredients of political innovation not derived from significant sectors of opinion in the education service, and willed upon society as a whole. The management of schools and services has to become politicised, in one sense or another. The school may uncritically and subserviently be passing on the intentions of legislation. It may be interpreting and selecting priorities within the shifting legal framework. It may be temporising and avoiding the direct intentions of state legislation, in the hope of future change. It may be disregarding or seeking to have changed what is seen as bad law. A school which follows any but the first of these paths will need the confidence of full commitment and support for what it is trying to do, from the local community and from other schools and services around it. Doubtless for all but the most quixotic among us, interpretation and selection within the legal framework is the most probable path. This set of political choices is part of the context of school management across boundaries and across cultures.

Applications

The future scene, then, is of modes of organisation capable of reflecting, harnessing and engendering change. Management is to be conceived as a core element in the teaching and learning process and not just in the organisations set up to promote learning. Political assumptions include participation and empowerment for the context of schooling as well as the internal transactions of schools. What in practice are the major applications of management disciplines?

We have to start at the particular points where people and perceptions have been and probably still are, before offering direction towards a process involving them in the whole of a future context. Part of this book will apply management strategies to the management of teaching and learning; to the rapidly changing shapes and perceptions of 'middle management' inside schools; to the management of institutions as a whole and across institutions; to the various facets of a local education service, however in the future conceived; and to the local community, again however perceived.

From those starting points, a shared involvement in the whole context both of learning experience and of resources will be explored and the question posed whether this, rather than the previous points of departure might be the pre-supposition for future development. This context will modify the perceptions of management skills most likely to be appropriate. These skills may be related to personal and group capability and self-management. They may be about working with other people and helping them to work more effectively . They will be about managing time and resources to the best purpose. They will be about running organisations and systems, developing them and changing them, relating them to a context of other organisations and systems. The context will include the future management of the teaching profession as a whole.

Another element in this book will be the consideration of the management skills most needed to make schools work towards goals which are likely to continue modified rather than altered, but in a context of change which will have transformed not only situations and learning needs but also the range of opportunities and modes of learning. It will, moreover, inform proposals and programmes for management development, much more broadly conceived than some of the compilations of managerial dominance seen in recent initiatives.

Current contexts

The particular prompting of such a book at this time is the general sense in our society of lost direction or retrogression, contradictory value systems, and organisational confusion, all of which are bound to affect the quality of learning experiences offered through an education service. The urgent need is not just for schools to be managed more effectively, but for society, including its teachers, to capture some common sense of what effect it wishes schools to have.

There has been a decade of disillusionment among teachers and around schools, leading to protracted industrial dispute and almost total breakdown of communication between the profession and governing politicians. The patched up compromises of conditions of service and salary structure, the plethora of government 'initiatives,' the short-sighted and incomplete 'reforms' of public examinations, the uneven and unworthy instruments of professional development and review, the eclipse of the national inspectorate and the uncertain future role of local authorities, the inadequacies and unpredictability of funding mechanisms are preoccupying most of the teaching profession. The education service is in no state to be able to make sense of any one of these unless it can rediscover in itself an open professionality through which to contribute to vision for society's future, and against which to measure the mixture of good and bad proposals which will continue to emerge from all quarters. The way schools are organised and governed cannot be divorced from the way a teaching profession is organised and governed. At the moment, it is neither organised nor governed at all. The quest for a general teaching council is directly related to our theme.

I shall make no apology for ranging from practical and specific school management problems to general issues affecting the whole community. It is precisely because these have not been adequately connected that there remains a major management problem to be resolved for the future of schooling. For many years, we have been echoing the war-time slogan, but uttered to some mythical 'you out there': give us the tools and we'll finish the job. Instead, we shall have to be proposing, to ourselves as a society of shared perceptions: give us the job, and we'll finish the tools.

TWO

Values and Management

The aim of management is not only the better running of institutions. Indeed, as soon as we choose static words like *institution, establishment,* or the *State,* or our own *status* or *position,* we are wrongly committed to an argument which is either about maintaining the status quo or about the physical forces, the dynamics, of change and we are pulled away from the human values and the being and becoming of life, which make up *organisations* and for which organisations exist.

In what sense could management be said to have an aim? There may well be principles and theories of management as there are principles or theories of movement, but not on the same plane of argument as the goal or direction or even the human motivation which prompt movement. Management, like movement, is neutral. The moral neutrality of management is not a matter of pride but of fact. I see principles of management more at the level of how a vehicle works, how to drive it, how to conduct oneself as a driver, than at the level of whether we should drive cars, whether we should all decide where to travel or for what purposes. So it should be viewed as a technology rather than as a fundamental science or body of theory or value system. It is about means. We cannot have means without ends, and should not be managing schools without ground rules. However, the ground rules are not internal to management, and we should be suspicious of management theory, not because it is theory but because it may be presented in its own right.

If there are underlying theories, value systems, or governing principles for this technology of management, they are derived from observation through a variety of disciplines: psychology, sociology, anthropology, and especially political and moral philosophy. Our problem is that the prevailing modes of each of these base disciplines may be in conflict, and that none of these has recently had the credibility or capability to inform and direct our society as a whole or the service which most obviously must look to its ground disciplines for guidance.

Psychology has become marginalised in the education service, partly because of the misguided attempt and failure to establish an exclusive sub-science of the kind which we may also find in management writings projected as science, and partly by the focus in educational psychology services on remediating failure to function rather than the central thrusts of curriculum, method and organisation. This problem is explored in some detail elsewhere (Jones and Sayer, 1988). Sociology has sometimes used our behaviour as illustration after the event for patterns and theories, although Eric Hoyle's recent book (1986) reminds us usefully of the perceptions of loosely coupled systems and could be a bridge towards political philosophy. Anthropology has been avoided as we hold our tribes to the rhetoric of individual nurture, even though the ethnographic, qualitative approaches to research and the concern for the culture and development of whole organisations has been valuable. Philosophy has lacked that capability of putting theory into practice which I would wish to see as the contribution of appropriate management. Our society is without a sufficient political consensus for schools to be managed towards a common purpose. In the resulting vacuum, which is not confined to the education service, some have been properly critical of management volumes which make means into ends, and ends into means.

We can see such things happening at a distance more easily than at home. So when in 1986 censored news stories were coming out of South Africa about the further wave of shootings in Soweto, we allowed ourselves to listen to the Deputy Minister of Information telling us that the issue was not about apartheid or the loss of life or the behaviour of the police or about school programmes, but about the overthrow of the State – as though this meant we should swallow loss of life and liberty, and preserve the institution whose only justification would be to preserve what was being destroyed. Much the same has been emanating from China in 1989. We find the same sort of language when schools or departments or local authorities or our own position are under threat of closure. It comes out, too, in some utterances from manufacturing industry or government, reminding us that unless there is a profit we cannot have schools, colleges or universities, so these should make economic profit an end in itself, equated with institutional survival. Jarratt's cost centres or schools managing their whole budget make good sense as a means of running a household, a ménage, a management unit, and enabling everyone involved to share in getting value for money; they make no sense at all if the money is equated with the value, in a market force sink or swim economy.

Too often, we dictate the journey by the nature of the car, or even invent journeys in order to justify having a car, a school, a service, a State, a personal position. The best way to escape from that trap of position-preserving dynamic inertia is to work on the fundamental thinking, the governing principles of human society and therefore of an education service. It is against these that we should measure such management desirables as clarity, effectiveness, use of human resources, recognition of achievement, or teamwork.

Keeping it simple

Schools by their survival against all the odds show up the shortcomings of management precept borrowed from single-purpose institutions. Charles Handy asks whether schools have to be so complicated (Handy, 1984); we can properly ask back whether life is all that simple. It is neither easy nor politically attractive to present the complexity of life and learning, or of school systems which try to take these into account; but there is also some truth in the view that those who simplify simply lie. And because we are about translating human values into practice, we may reject, if it is there to be rejected, Handy's assertion that 'To a manager there may not always be time to develop the weak or the means to shape the situation to the individual. In management the greater good of the greater number can drive out the minority.' It will be a shared value system, not the practice of management, which will determine whether or not the weakest go to the wall.

Instead of registering that management which, like the motor car, is in itself valueless, we should be agreeing goals, and then we have to equip ourselves to head towards them; if we have values, it is no good just proclaiming them, we have to find ways to put them into practice. Too often education has proclaimed values and outcomes which are not reflected in what has actually been happening; and we then lay ourselves open to just the mindless valueless simplistic short-term narrow and specific targeting for expediency which has trapped the weakly democratic systems of our society as a whole.

Effectiveness

School effectiveness is a current management preoccupation; but effectiveness for what? We have been reminded recently (White, 1987) of Alasdair MacIntyre's view (1981) that it is dangerous to focus on being effective, since the contrivance of means involves the manipulation of human beings into compliant behaviour. MacIntyre's argument is a weak one. Effectiveness or ineffectiveness can be applied to protest, revolution or change, just as much as it can to screwing an audience to their seats. It can be applied by a whole

17

group interacting, not just by one person manoeuvring others. Do we just not want human values to be put into practice? Do we not want to dirty our hands? Do we want just to be able to protest without having the capability to change and improve? As for manipulation (a word which, incidentally, has nothing to do with management), well, that may also be what puts my back straight, with my agreement and cooperation.

It may, however, rightly be asked whose are the values which are to be translated into effective practice? That presents problems not just in a society clinging on to the apparatus of dead values, but in multicultural setting too. The problem is not just for managing an institution; it is about society as a whole. The challenge is to work out management principles which will enable different people and their different value systems to be an asset to each other. That has to be worked out not by a select breed of managers, but by the whole community. Those who have management skills have the job of sharing them. That means management training for all. But if management is about means and applications, those statements require underwriting outside the scope of management, which could not be expected alone to be the harbinger of ethics.

Using people

There are objections raised to writers on management who may be found treating personal qualities as instrumental. I see nothing wrong with that in itself. What is wrong is having no value system within which personal qualities can be used; it is wrong to treat personal qualities as *merely* instrumental. It is wrong to use people as a means beyond their own ends. But if people, in all their variety, and their participation in decision making are of the essence, then it is entirely appropriate for us all to share in identifying and drawing on personal qualities and capabilities. Indeed, it would be foolish not to, as well as degrading to those who have a contribution to make to worthwhile activity.

What is objectionable is the abuse and replacement of mutually respecting human relationships: for example, with the device of calculated praise by those in charge of an enterprise, not as one human being wanting to express pleasure at what another is doing, but just to keep the workers 'happy' or compliant without being able to comment back. By all means, let everyone be 'stroking' each other, if we mean it, and let us create in schools a society in which we can share and enjoy each other's achievements. That way, the medium fits the message. That is a far cry from patronising behaviour, which belongs to the boss mentality.

Equally objectionable is what the Germans call Bonbon-Pädagogik:

offering rewards or goodies for doing something you would otherwise not want to do. Whether that is praise, title, certification, or bonus, it is part of a slave culture, and in the long run it just will not work among thinking people. So, for example, having made teaching so much less attractive than, say, accountancy, we cannot bribe and buy ourselves out of bad long-term planning and managerial incompetence, by offering mathematics and physics graduates first qualification without training, or now that has gone, extra money either to train or to teach, or even a licence to teach without qualification.

The values taken into school management must include recognition of human dignity, self-respect and self-esteem. A democratic respect for human dignity includes the individual's moral responsibility for action. But there is the problem of moving away from the self-esteem of the kind Pat White (1987) describes as a 'collection of overblown egos'. On management courses, as in any group activity, one of the most challenging problems for all concerned is the individual who may well be high on self-esteem, and confidence, but whose self-esteem is ill-founded, or is more apparent than real. This may well have been brought on by the hierarchical systems and expectations which are the reality if not the language of our school culture, or it may have developed as a protective crust, or both. I am reminded of the question: Are pompous people appointed to headship or does headship make them pompous? But it is the whole ladder of individual success and failure at school, (which school?), individual success or failure in exams, Oxbridge or emergency trained, hierarchies of subject specialism, wanting to be top of the class or top of the school or top of the service, this particular view of *achievement* as the winning streak, (another objectionable management title); it is the expectation among selectors that this is what leadership should be about, and that anything else is second best, that we are having to question. And frankly, if you have been put in that position of assumed semi-divine omnipotence and acted that way for any time, it is fiendishly difficult to kick the habit.

Individual and corporate self-respect

A group of people confident in their respect for others can enable an individual to take stock, have another look, identify the problem, perhaps share it and build on the sharing, outside the context of threat to status and position, to see status and position as themselves the real threat. But that requires corporate self-respect in a group, without which individual self-respect cannot properly exist or be fostered. Winnie Mandela's self-respect would, I imagine, make little sense to her if she had not been sharing, representing and articulating the sufferings of other people; and self-respect cannot easily be sustained once these other people cease for whatever reason to identify with it.

꙼ I have dwelt on this corporate self-respect because it seems to me to be the most urgent immediate issue for the education service to consider. Individual teachers have been moving out of the profession because they have been affected and profoundly wounded by a *corporate* loss of self-respect. That is not going to be reversed by a rise in salary or birth-rate or the price of a barrel of oil. It will require a total rebuild of this great public service, from its foundations, not just from a puff of white smoke from the chimney stack. It will have to come from groups organising themselves, from teamwork and corporate respect as the basis of organisation, from an open professionality confident to share responsibility and therefore able to influence what happens in society as a whole. It is from that kind of cellular growth that I would wish to see responsibility, representation, school governance and local government take on a new meaning, more akin to the democratic ideals which we proclaim. And it is in that context of corporate self-respect that we need for the whole service a General Teaching Council with the confidence to open outwards.

Teamwork requires an appropriate approach to managing. Management has been closely, and I believe wrongly, associated with a particular kind of society and a particular kind of individualism. Individual achievement, opportunity, performance, capability, effectiveness, efficiency, viability, accountablity, growth, success are not necessarily the moral values which we would wish to uphold, but these have been the hallmarks of what has been described as good management.

Achievement

There have been many voices raised in protest against the very principle of achievement, the German *Leistungsprinzip*. Bertrand de Jouvenel (1963) points to the reaction of indigenous cultures during a period of colonisation, and to the continuing conflict in Third World countries between the struggle to raise so-called living standards in conflict with their own traditions. There is the obvious conflict within Christian cultures of, on the one hand, love of neighbour, lilies in the field, two or three gathered together with the leadership among them; and on the other, of Mankind set above the rest of nature and aiming to dominate it, or the Protestant work ethic, which we are not quite sure whether to change for ourselves. Labriola (1959) saw the will towards technical dominance, when it could be considered in a European context, as a Nordic rather than a Mediterranean characteristic. Marxism accepted its own form of *Leistungsprinzip*, in working to overthrow the managers. And De Jouvenel comments:

> The principle of achievement is instrumental in nature: to organise resources according to a stated aim in order to realise it as fully as possible. But how are we to determine the aim? Can the principle of achievement be raised to become a transcendental principle? If we reject all cultural values, then we have no other criteria by which to evaluate. All we can strive to achieve is the development of power. By power we generally mean the ability to bring about what we want; but what we want is again dependent on the values we recognise; without the existence of recognised values, only naked power remains as the object of our will. This is the reversal of all values: to see power not as a means to realise what makes sense, and only to accept as good sense what serves to develop power.

Self-centredness and self-realisation have been seen by others as being in conflict with group cultures, with care, protection, adjustment, and recognition. The trend among young people since the 1960s towards group or communal living of one kind or another, whether community service or alternative living or both, is seen not just as a passing reaction against a rat-race society, but as expressing an elemental human need. Teamwork in learning, in research, in T-groups, in group protest, depends on and fosters the mutual trust and respect on which democracy may be constantly renewed; whereas we may consider some attempts to promote competition in schools, not least by the banks, as a frantic attempt to stoke up competitiveness for its own sake.

Values of learning

The study of learning, or learning how we learn, is assumed to be a base discipline for education, even if educational psychology has been isolated and marginalised, and even if the agenda for school change seems to omit altogether how people can best learn. If we examine what value is attached to learning as a human activity, this may inform and perhaps re-form and re-cast the other debate about the way schools are run.

This is not one of those moments in human history when it seems that all human activity and social organisation have been directed towards the extension of ideas, or knowledge, or the discovery of divine truths. There are still traces of all these in human activity today; more, perhaps in the rhetoric than in the reality of our existence, when *homo rapiens* has so conspicuously replaced *homo sapiens*.

It is in our more recent context of the economic performance of competing nations that organised learning or education has emerged

21

as a mass phenomenon. It is sometimes not clear whether the earlier traditions of truth, beauty and justice remain ends in themselves or are included when they provide a justification for power. There has always been, as there is now, a tension between the human and other values and the corporate or private interests which between them prompt and persuade action. Politics is a branch of philosophy as well as a system of management.

Up to a point, which is perhaps the point at which affluence dampens the drive for survival, there remains the faith that learning is natural, a basic human appetite; but there are gaps of perception about the nature of learning. Sometimes, it is the process of discovery, sometimes the outcome; sometimes it is the acquisition of knowledge, sometimes a resulting change of behaviour. Usually, we are content to leave it as a mix of all of these. If learning is a basic human activity, then we talk of education as a fundamental human right. Again, we have to decide what we actually mean. Do we mean the right to be subjected to behavioural change? Or in what sense and for whom is compulsory education a right? For a society, for parents or for children? It may be seen as the right of a society to impose education on its young or on any other grouping, in order to maintain the fabric of that society. It may be a right of access, requiring a society and parents to provide for the young what is rightfully theirs by virtue of being human beings? Or it may be an entitlement for parents to have their children educated according to their wishes and beliefs.

It may follow from whatever the answer may be that a national curriculum is required of schools or that it is required of pupils. If education is established as a means to create national wealth, then there will be an emphasis on acquiring and developing specifically defined and requisite skills, which individuals are required to have. If society's wealth is to promote the progress of humanity, then wealth is acquired as a means towards education in the broadest sense, and schools are accountable to learners for translating a nation's wealth into learning opportunity.

Education and learning are not the same. Education as a provided commodity is measured in outcomes, in terms of what can be demonstrated to have been learned; learning, on the other hand, is judged as good or bad according to whether it seems to have improved a person's quality of life, culture and education in a personal sense, or whether it has damaged it. We have come to use the word education more and more as tangibly given and received, recognised and institutionalised. We cannot assume that education, most recognisably provided through the medium of schools, results in learning valuable to the person. Indeed, we have no right to assume what kind of learning occurs.

What kind of learning is wanted?

People learn in different ways. Some of the differences are induced. Set a group a series of problem-solving exercises without laying down the ground rules, and some will plunge in as individuals, determined to be first home, not least because that is the way they have been taught by their school system. Others, similarly competitive with the same task, will check first, find that the time taken is of no account, and will concentrate on getting it right, with the assumption that the level of perfection in the completed task is what will count, and not the speed of their achievement. Some will work together, helping each other, and will derive satisfaction from a group achievement. A different kind of group satisfaction emerges if the problem-solving group or team perceives itself to be in competition with another group. In each instance, it is difficult to judge what is the prime motivation: to solve the problem, to demonstrate the ability to do so, or to show as the best performer or performing group.

All or any of these modes of learning activity can be trained. Which of them is of greatest value to the society which sets up schools? We come across a variety of responses. One is that recognition should be given to the different ways in which people learn, and that programmes of study should be of mixed methodology, so that there is something there for everyone. That is either resigned agnosticism or a lazy-minded form of liberalism; it is the wisest course if we know that we do not know, and if we can respect and tolerate people's different propensities without having to form value judgments. Another approach is to try to find out how people best learn, and adapt our methods and learning opportunities accordingly. We have been trying that for a century and making mistakes as we go. Another is to distinguish between the learning process and content, and to adopt an attitude that there are so many valuable things to learn that it does not much matter which of them we choose as content: what matters is the nature and quality of the learning experience. Not knowledge for knowledge's sake, but learning for learning's sake. So we vacillate between didactic and experiential modes of learning, between individual and group approaches, between competitive and cooperative modes. On the whole, it is the structured, didactic, mass approach to competing individuals which prevails in the reality of schools and classrooms and is reinforced in regulations, whilst the rhetoric of good practice is about enabling experiential, group and cooperative learning activity. The most recent political moves suggest more still of the former; the most recent pedagogies are about the latter. The legislated school system and the practice of learning are set against one another. Young people perceive that the value systems of school and society are at odds, and are all the less likely to be motivated to learn.

If we do not agree what kind of learning should be promoted, the skills of those who focus on learning skills are diverted to the single area of agreement: that those who find special difficulty in learning should be helped. Learning support systems are largely based on the individual pupil. Even worse, they have been applied almost exclusively to individual malfunctions and deficits. Educational psychology has become a branch of plumbing: the unblocking of drains. Its connection with school management is largely confined to instances of crisis and breakdown. These instances are largely confined to individual cases. These, in turn, are individual pupils.

Psychology, as practised generally in the education service, is not seen as part of organisation management. The further pupils are embedded in the school structure, the less is the educational psychologist involved in the process. Secondary schools and further education are alien territory. Most of the school system established to promote learning is out of touch with the study of how people learn, and unable to relate learning skills and settings to the purposes of a school's existence, whether those purposes are economic, social, or philosophical.

Where economic values predominate and learning is measured by quantified knowledge outcomes, and if a society wishes principally to increase its total store of knowledge and capability, the most effective way may be to focus on the most effective learners, whose knowledge increases by leaps and bounds, far outstripping the progress of the average or less than average performer. That might mean organising a school by streaming and concentrating resources on top streams, or by pitching the work in mixed-ability groups to the level of the above average.

This may be modified if a society gives priority to cheap ways of spreading knowledge widely; there may be a cascade model, such as that adopted at the beginning of the nineteenth century by Bell (1797) and then Lancaster (1803), or adopted by Sir Keith Joseph's ministry in supporting the training of heads to be trainers.

If, on the other hand, social harmony and cohesiveness is the principal aim, team-learning may become an end in itself. Well managed, it can also be argued as the best instrument for making progress on courses, not just for the group as a whole, but for each individual member. Even if it were not, given the priorities, teamwork would remain the basis of learning programmes. Group rewards for the achievement of the whole group may have positive effects on individual learning, but competition between groups detracts from the advantages of building on other groups' progress.

Mutual respect between teachers and learners, adults and the young will represent another dimension of human and social values. This may show in various ways, with groups and with individuals. Pupils and teachers are active partners in learning. The teacher is appointed as group leader. Tasks and roles have to be negotiated if the group is to be more than the sum of its members. In finding out how well pupils are achieving, teachers will wish to find out how pupils think they are achieving.

Consensus is not the whole story. It may be an outcome. However, schools which avoid controversy are robbing pupils of learning opportunities. *Glasnost* should prevail; differences of opinion should be aired; classrooms ought to be places of dispute and conflict. Schools should present challenges. Making mistakes is necessary for learning. If failure is blamed on lack of ability or bad luck, it will not be a spur for further effort. Teachers should convince failing pupils that they can succeed if they try harder. If teachers show patronising sympathy for the disadvantaged, they reduce these pupils' belief in themselves. It may even be argued that teachers who show anger are showing they believe that pupils can do better, and may spur pupils to greater effort.

These are issues which have to be faced if schools are in the business of learning. The responses depend on the choice of a basis of social psychology: human behaviour as influenced by others. That is the basis of work that goes on in schools and classrooms, which are social units and contain smaller social units within them.

Grouping policies are rare in schools, beyond expressions of belief in mixed-ability sets or streams. Yet group learning is at the heart of a school's existence. Each individual has unique attributes, and these should be the basis of grouping policies, so that individuals can develop through their particular and positive contributions to groups. Achievement should belong not to the individual but to the whole learning group. There are various levels at which concepts and practice of the psychology of groupwork should be pursued. There are techniques which can be acquired and chosen consciously by teachers and learners. They may include the 'jigsaw' team-learning technique, in which each member of a group is assigned a part of a task to learn and then to teach to the rest of the group; or team-assisted individualisation; or structured controversy within a cooperative context. Also, there are aspects of attribution of success and failure: causality and motivation; the capacity to do something about what may be side-effects to some and major effects to others. Using these, the social effects of school groupings and group procedures on gender, race and creed, or the background effects of gender, race and creed on learning and group relation habits in the classroom have to be seen as a major responsibility in schools.

There are further consequences for the main channels of professional preparation and practice. One is the initial preparation of teachers. Teacher-training has to be about group skills, about cooperative contexts, about using group differences to create valuable learning. Much of teacher training, including in-service development, should not only be *about* groupwork; it should consist of group experiences. If group learning has advantages, teachers should be enabled to develop programmes and policies in heterogeneous groups, not just to encourage their pupils to do so. There is more to collegiality than salary scales and contractual responsibility.

How does GCSE fit such an approach? Frankly, not at all. It merely reinforces the competitive dissonance which on psychological and social grounds ought to be reduced in favour of cooperative modes of behaviour. It is not just the individual basis of reward and recognition which is fundamentally objectionable; some forms of group recognition are equally damaging and distracting. Achievement should be directed to and measured against the completion of negotiated tasks, not against other groups. Yet schools are now being encouraged or forced to compete for custom, with no regard for models of inter-group relationships and cooperation towards superordinate goals; the insights of psychology have yet to penetrate political or educational policy making.

What sort of achievement is valuable? Mark Twain once asked why it was that prisoners making bags was thought to be work, whilst scaling Mont Blanc was seen as sport. Both are achievements; but the prisoners were making bags because someone else had told them to; climbing Mont Blanc is felt to be an achievement because the climbers had the choice and decided to do it themselves. We may have shifted from the direct slave or feudal compulsion to a society of indirect compulsion through dependency on reward or wages, but for a sense of achievement in having done something worthwhile, worth working and living for, we still have the task of reducing what is determined by others, and enhancing self-determined responsible achievement, through reducing rank, privilege and discrimination, and through working towards freedom and equality. Our problem, in an education service as in the society it serves to improve, is that democracy cannot thrive if it is less effective than tyranny. And that is why, again, I would want to see a management technology as philosophy in practice.

For the issue is not just about management, nor should it be. It is about the political philosophy of education: about ends and means, about society and the individual, authority and responsibility, and the value of human beings. It is about Macchiavelli and Hobbes, or about Locke and Mill; about the divine right of kings, or *vox populi vox dei*; about the rule and dictate of right reason, or about reasons of state, Realpolitik, and pragmatism. It is about the democratisation of the whole education service, if it is to serve appropriately to foster and if necessary reform a democratic society; or it is about power, of the kind which Bertrand Russell (1932) predicted and of the kind which Hannah Arendt (1986) experienced before moving to her recent conclusion about human groups and a new basis for society.

Political thought now has to be transferred from its pre-nineteenth-century forms into the concerns which now prevail and preoccupy; not just throne and altar, or elected assembly of the nation-state. Take the management decisions about atomic energy, acid rain, chemical sprays, pesticides or fertilisers. Criteria for decision making have to include international acceptability; social acceptability including cultural values; environmental acceptability now that at last we are aware that *homo sapiens* cannot continue as *homo rapiens*; and also economic viability.

These are more likely to be the great curricular issues of the coming age than are the dosages and diets of content material which are going to preoccupy the politics of education in the next decade. How these are approached in the management of schools will depend on the values and priorities we attach to the processes of learning. Management is about putting all these together and organising to do something about it; interpreting in action a democratic equivalent of philosopher-kingship; and it has both to draw on a range of disciplines, and to put them into effect.

That is just as true of an education service, not just as a preparation for democracy but as a major component. To embody and foster and if need be to discover the values of society, it ought to be offering pointers to good practice beyond its own management. To query prestige limousines or helicopters in other enterprises, it ought to address its own trivial and obvious and sometimes absurd rituals: why heads and chiefs of service have their own parking space or their own loo; why HMI graduate from plastic to leather brief-cases, from floor to floor, size of room, carpet, desk and chair; whether students and staff enjoy similar facilities; why in a vast service with a majority of women, only a few are chief education officers – we all have our lists of glaring discrepancies, sometimes mere symbols and gestures which speak volumes about the real nature of our relationships and values.

Our relationship with other services should be the same respecting mutuality which we have to foster across our profession and across teachers and learners, schools and communities. Our problem in fearing that wrong-minded management practices may be foisted upon us is that we have not developed the practice of that corporate self-respect or sense of shared purpose which enables us to discriminate useful learning from management clutter. We have to be confident in order to be active learners from good practice elsewhere. That confidence can only come from having responsibility for developing and marketing our own good practice. Instead of just borrowing or rejecting management practices from other cultures, or being ripped off, the education service as a major element of organised society has to become capable of offering examples of management practice appropriate to shared values, and has to be able to show other enterprises that values can be make to work, how they work, and why they should be made to work not just in an education service but in any activity sustained by and sustaining a society which inclines towards democracy.

THREE

Change and Arrest

Introduction

Everyone is in favour of change. Everyone, with William Blake, expects poison from standing waters. But everyone is also in favour of consolidation, of uninterrupted sequences through which to complete what has been started, of being left to get on with a job. The most recent HMI report on secondary schools echoes dissatisfaction with the state of many schools; but its plea is for stability and security:

> Schools have faced in recent years demands and advice from a bewildering variety of sources: government departments, LEAs, examination boards, universities, parents, pressure groups, industry, teachers' associations (both their professional bodies and subject-teacher groups), and inspectors and advisers. At times these have had a common thrust and have looked towards generally agreed objectives but often the objectives and the priorities afforded them have varied and even conflicted sharply. And often the speed of change demanded has been much too brisk. In these circumstances, it is hardly surprising that schools have not always welcomed the imposition of change or known in which direction to move . . . If schools are to feel confident in moving forward, they urgently need a measure of stability, public support and improved morale and also a sense of nationally shared purpose and commitment. (HMI, 1988)

But abjectly, HMI, having themselves become part of a slave culture, offer the imposed national curriculum as a solution, as though it were shared.

There is a vast difference between change engendered from within organisations, and imposed alterations. Too often, the persuasive arguments for change as a way of life are left as a creed by which we delude ourselves into perpetuating the past. More frequently still, as part of the self-delusory art of politics, the gad-fly habit persuades us that we are the agents of change, whilst the efforts are being made in spite of our irritating noises and stings. So the effect of the HMI report on the Secretary of State was inevitably to tell schools they

29

must do better rather than indulge in public self-scrutiny or to take the advice of the text.

Organisations which make changes in isolation from their context may cause powers to be transferred to another which is less susceptible to change. Curriculum development in schools may start with the expectation of informing and transforming public examinations, but becomes delimited by them; or public examinations may begin to move with the times, but are then taken over by an even more conservative central government department; or participative democracy may be so fully developed that power has to be removed to a safely distant location, as appears to happen in West German schools and in British higher education.

This chapter, therefore, examines the contrasts and ironies of change and arrest in the schools system. This is particularly prompted by the 1980–88 legislation which in Britain could bring the school system to a destabilised standstill, or could shake down into an unpredictable pattern and spectrum of change unlikely to be related to identified future needs.

Future change

Looking at human society in the round, it appears to be rational to work on some or all of the following assumptions:

(a) that social, political and economic development will be more internationally than nationally determined;
(b) that the practices and social effects of labour-intensive and plant-oriented nineteenth-century industrial economies will be replaced by those of high technology human scale operation;
(c) that general purpose representative government (or periodically elected general programme dictatorship) will be replaced by participative democracy strengthened by instant communication on specific issues;
(d) that established hierarchies of power and privilege, whether founded on birth, wealth or monopolised knowledge, will be replaced by skills applied to problem solving and information networked for accessibility to all;
(e) that established career development, leisure and unemployment patterns will be replaced by more flexible, less secure and more self-determined work habits and interludes;
(f) that organisations will be more about programmes than about institutions;
(g) that decision-making activity will be open to a complex of contexts and alternatives; that these will reduce the notion of 'levels' of decision making by encroaching on them all;
(h) that the inter-connectedness of activities affecting the same

people will be reflected in the way those activities are worked out together;

(*i*) that management patterns which were suitable for more static, secure, hierarchical, isolated organisations will need to be modified;

(*j*) that the pace of discovery and change will continue to accelerate so that it becomes the habit and expectation;

(*k*) that change and discovery will not be harnessed to growth and profit but to sharing and reduction of need for scarce planetary resources.

In educational terms, these assumptions might lead to:

(*a*) access to the languages, cultures and development needs of the whole human race, whether located locally or elsewhere in the world village; a reduction in skills and priorities harnessed to national supremacy;

(*b*) progressive movement from the factory model of schooling to the use of information resources located in homes and other social centres, with personal and small group tutorial transactions replacing mass instruction;

(*c*) exercise of multiple skills in specific project-based learning activity rather than lowest common denominator balanced content-diet prescriptions;

(*d*) sharing and rotations of responsibility according to skills required for particular activities; teamwork combining skills replacing individual positional power;

(*e*) reinterpretation of age-related compulsory education as lifelong learning intermeshed with work and leisure, with particular early childhood and third age emphases;

(*f*) education relating to people and tasks, rather than to established norms or authority based on previous work patterns;

(*g*) a basic educational right of access to information networks and the skill to use them; strategic decision making brought closer to points of activity;

(*h*) connections with other organisational cultures and patterns, and the ability to develop inter-team cooperative activity in education and all related services;

(*i*) progressive replacement of classical bureaucratic organisations, whether in the local education service or in its wider systems, by more participative models;

(*j*) the habit for new task groups to form according to demands and new priorities, replacing position and tenure in particular establishments;

(*k*) environmental nurture as the key science, with educational practice giving priority to reduced expenditure of natural resource and the most cost-effective use of natural and human energy.

In management terms, these long-term strategic assumptions might suggest for the education service:

(a) an emphasis on language, cultural interchange, human rights and development education;
(b) primacy for the tutorial role of teachers in the community;
(c) a diachronic and progressive view of curricular breadth and balance related to the whole range of learning experience and not confined to a daily or weekly school diet or even necessarily to a particular age phase;
(d) constant task-related staff development policies and strategies for the education service;
(e) community education as the basis of an organised service, with plant and facilities related to community-wide and lifelong learning;
(f) within a secure framework of entitlement, learning programmes organised by client negotiation by a mobile and flexible service;
(g) local decision making with computer-assisted administration helping to mobilise resources and with communication systems strengthened within and across local schools, services and the community;
(h) the primacy of team management and 'managing outwards' to combine teams from different services;
(i) corporate management at the points of service delivery as the apex of specific professional or funding systems;
(j) task-oriented network systems of management in a context of collegiality within and across services;
(k) the technologies of environmental care and economic use of resources at the heart of educational programmes and the way they are organised.

To these may then be added changes which are *desired* and determined within the framework or parameters of managing according to what is likely to happen anyway. These may vary from one country to another, from one regional or local circumstance to another, from one political tendency to another. Services should be so organised that they are capable of anticipating and adapting the parameters of a society's decision making as well as helping each society to adapt to those changes likely to affect us all.

Relevance of recent legislation

Set against such priorities for management, the recent legislation in Britain appears to have the following effects:

(a) There are no signs in the legislation between 1980 and 1988 of emphasis on development education or cultural interchange.

There is some emphasis on a modern foreign language, to be specified by government order, to be part of the school programme from the age of eleven to sixteen; there are however fears that it will be more difficult to include other languages in the time which remains unprescribed. Despite Britain being a party to human rights declarations through the United Nations and through the Council of Europe, the legislation neither provides for education as a right nor does it provide for education to promote human rights; rather, it is to be about education to reach expected standards. Compare the 1792 declaration by Romme to the national convention in France:

> It is between these two scales of our knowledge and our needs that all citizens of any age and either sex, exercising their natural powers, and progressing freely and gradually shall be able on the one hand to acquire stage by stage new intellectual capacities, and on the other to apply them for their own benefit or for the public good. The level at which any individual shall stop in this career shall be the one which nature has herself registered as the limit of the individual's powers. Any other obstacle would be an affront to the right of every citizen to acquire all those perfections of which he or she is capable.

(b) The use of the word community as presented in the 1944 Education Act has been abandoned. It is mentioned in the 1988 Act only in relation to the governance of those schools which opt for nationalisation, that is, for 'grant-maintained' status. There is no legislation during the period for adult and community education. Specific community provision such as the urban aid programme has been made separately. The need for teachers to be aware of the range of social backgrounds from which pupils are drawn is, however, recognised in the requirements for initial teacher education.

(c) The recent legislation has not come to terms with curriculum managed in any sense beyond the subjects on a school timetable with short-term objectives of meeting standards measured by tests.

(d) The conditions of service imposed in the 1987 legislation require a minimum of five days per school year to be allocated to in-service training; the management of INSET is harnessed through the grant-related in-service training schemes which the 1988 legislation enables the government to control; and the same legislation empowers the government to introduce a formal staff appraisal scheme for teachers.

(e) The organisation of community education does not figure in recent legislation; it does pay lip-service to the training of governors.

(*f*) Only the 1981 Act makes any attempt to secure a framework of entitlement for a minority with special educational needs. The same Act is the only one to give some formal role to parents in negotiating responses to needs; it has been shown not to be working as intended, and could be further jeopardised by the indirect effects of the 1988 Education Reform Act's amalgam of strait-laced curriculum, testing, local financial management and open enrolment.

(*g*) The 1980 Act gave more emphasis to access to information and to governing bodies than had been practised in many local authorities; the role and composition of governing bodies and their connection with formal meetings of parents was broadened in the 1986 legislation; the 1986 and 1988 legislation extends the role of governors in appointing staff; the 1988 legislation extends their role in relation to resource management, but takes back to central government much of the ultimate responsibility for curriculum; government funds earmarked for microcomputing in schools have been largely directed at computer-assisted learning rather than administration.

(*h*) The recent legislation emphasises choice of institution and individual school governance and management; it appears to be inimical to inter-school cooperative provision. The emphasis is on individual performance, whether of pupils or of teachers, and not on teamwork. The 1981 Act includes reference to other services, but is not binding upon them.

(*i*) The legislation from 1980–88 has moved administrative responsibility to the points of individual service delivery; the only significant reference to local inter-service collaboration is the consultation on curriculum with the local police; there is no equivalent injunction on the police.

(*j*) Classical management models of bureaucracy, hierarchy and separate islands of management are strengthened by the laws of the 1980s.

(*k*) Cost-effectiveness is being emphasised, though not for the reasons suggested above. Local financial management does bring with it direct responsibility for the use of resources and can be wedded to energy conservation schemes. The accountability model being applied is not yet related to educational criteria.

So only in (*d*) (staff development), (*g*) (local communication and management) and potentially (*k*) (local financial management) does current legislation appear to take minor steps in the direction which would make any sense for the future. In all other respects, it either neglects or runs counter to global aims which might appear to be rational and management practices which would help to achieve them. It does not change the system, but arrests it. This presents a real dilemma for those who want to make sense of running schools.

Waves of reaction

Most teachers and parents have kept very quiet while government has been pursuing the quirks of reform through legislation. Should we have taken to the barricades to prevent the clearest attempt to subvert the work of the last seventy years from the Fisher Report? Or treat the whole decade of politicking with cold distant contempt? The truth is, 'we' do not exist; a tiny group of activists has had more effect on the government's behaviour than half a million trained and practising educators and the representatives of ten million parents. The large groups of educators have been too much at odds among themselves and also too honest to pretend that all was for the best in the best of all possible worlds. The small single-purpose group has recognised the reality of an elective dictatorship, of the slave courtier culture which gets things done, or working the media as conviction absorbed by rote, of simple thrusts.

The education service has not known what to do about it other than play for time, waiting for rescue acts from some electoral accident which would have as little to do with education as did the results of the last round. The political challenge to the education service from 1976 on was perhaps misguided, but by political standards honourable enough. The changes made in educational legislation straight after 1979 – choice of school, information on exam results and sex education, assisted places to swing back from the ending of direct grant, and changes to governing bodies – were tempered by a proper concern not to subvert the schools service: choice was within a planning framework, disclosure within the whole picture offered by schools, assisted places at least supposed to be allowed only where the system was otherwise inadequate; the language and notions of cooperative partnership were maintained until the mid-1980s.

That has gone, as have the consensus politics without which it is difficult for schools to have or to give direction. Disputes, however started or fuelled, drove out anything from dialogue to honest agonising to understand. Britain, more than most developed countries, is stretching the scope of a market economy. The government view appears to be that if choice, either by individual parents or by individual schools, destabilises the system, well and good. If it strengthens the private sector at the expense of the public service, that is politically attractive. If it leads to segregation by race, creed, class, wealth, motivation or ability, that is perhaps a pity, but if it is what people want, that is that.

What the statutory education service knows least about in the market economy is the business of marketing. If you do not have a monopoly and are not in short supply, you have to market and sell. That does not just mean presenting yourself well, dressed up in pleasant brochures and vestibules and welcoming smiles; it means creating a need for your wares, and if the need does not exist, you create it. Invent a vacuum to fill.

There is only one effective marketing agency to do with education, and that is the Independent Schools Information Service. But what of professional ethics, of cooperation across schools? What of the scruples about competing for custom, of survival at the expense of those who may be giving their all to teaching rather than selling? Professional ethics depend on a common view among teachers and those that are there to serve that teaching is a profession anyway, or something more than a centrally directed slave trade, in the business of the survival of the fittest for the fittest by the fittest. Outside education, 10–15 per cent of an organisation's expenditure would be expected to be allocated to marketing and selling. The private sector of education took to emulating other business practice by the late 1970s, when it was clear that the trends were away from private to public education, and equally clear than an incoming government would provide opportunities to reverse that trend.

The more 'choice' is projected at the public, the less choice is permitted to individual schools. The national curriculum, like national health treatment, is to be controlled for political reasons, not for educational or medical ones. Curriculum and examinations, development and research, pay and conditions of service have all been secured by the central government's Department of Education and Science. The obvious desire to be seen by Downing Street to be in total control of the public service may be directed as much at the Departments of Employment, Trade and Industry, and the Environment as out to the teaching service or parents.

So what is to be done about it? There are oddities in the 1988 Act which politicians and those who have their ear may concede should be amended and which may be ironed out in regulations; but the education service has already spent too much time in the last ten years just reacting against political intervention, and reactive argument has not only fallen on ears known to be deaf before the shouting began; it has become an excuse for not getting on with some hard thinking and action about the important issues of future education and the long-term needs of society, most of which are ignored in the legislation. The problem becomes most acute where the government is calling a halt to any development work but its own; and in the 1988 legislation there is a clear injunction upon schools not to develop curricula unless sanctioned by the Secretary of State, nor to prepare for examinations other than those approved by the Secretary of State. Here we have the clearest signs of arrest at the heart of the system, under the banner of change. It is little comfort to be persuaded that this is bad law and unenforceable.

It may still be best so to change the debate that the current legislation is as marginalised as it deserves to be. Outright opposition is more likely to strengthen resolve to force nonsenses through. The problem is by no means unique to education or to a particular political position. Drucker's general view of managing in a political environment will find echoes in schools, despite the male language which still pervades much industrial management:

> The shift from consensus to confrontation and from the search for the common denominator to single-purpose fanaticism means that the traditional ways in which managers operated in the political arena will no longer work . . . the advice has always been: stay close to the politician . . . but it is no longer enough. One cannot appease the paranoid; the attempt only confirms his [sic] suspicions. Today's manager can no longer confine himself to reacting; he has to act. He can no longer wait; he must take the initiative and become an activist.

> The new manager . . . will be effective only if he ceases to see himself – and to be seen – as representing a 'special interest' . . . And then he has to become the proponent, the educator, the advocate. (Drucker, 1980)

This is a dangerous situation, and an even more dangerous remedy. In conflict situations, it is all too easy to take on the paranoia seen on the other side, or to become megalomaniac in taking over from government. What remains a matter of great concern in the longer term is that the Government by its behaviour has forfeited any claim to be taken seriously or to make a serious contribution to the nation's future education or to the morale of its educators. If it has turned from using its professional eyes and ears to deciding what it wants to see and hear, that and nothing besides, it may be more productive for educators to concentrate on other channels for public debate.

In this book, I am offering instead a dual approach. First, there are some aspects of current government trends which can be made to coincide with real improvements related to the development of management in schools: staff development, communication, local governance and local management of resources. Secondly, there are other key areas which have to be developed anyway, either marginalising the effect of recent legislation or circumventing it, if education is to meet future needs beyond the scope of short-term legislation or a particular political perception. In both these approaches, the skills in managing change and the management of conflict are crucial.

Educative change

This book started with the aim of reducing the gap between the management of learning and the management of the system to promote learning. Attempts by government to impose change on school systems are as unrealistic as attempts made by schools to impose behavioural change and learning on pupils. Teachers and parents find themselves in the same position as reluctant pupils, either 'creeping like snails unwillingly to school' or reacting and refusing.

Real change comes about from shared commitment, from negotiation and partnership in learning. It is that same partnership and shared understanding and commitment which has to be sought in the management of schools. A government which brushes aside anything but its own conviction and prescriptions may be likened to a teacher or a school which neither seeks nor permits comment from pupils or parents on its programmes. Equally, if we are to uphold the notion of shared responsibility, a profession which refuses the whole of a government programme because it has been imposed puts itself in the position of a pupil refusing the whole of schooling without being able to distinguish between what is worthwhile anyway, despite being compulsory, and what should be questioned, which may include the whole issue of compulsion.

In a typically illuminating and refreshing little article, Edward de Bono once distinguished between four types of management behaviour, offering the images of the train-driver, the farmer, the doctor and the fisher. He was suggesting that management training in Britain was quite good in preparing the first three, but weak with the fourth. The train-driver is characterised as having a set task to perform on given lines within prescribed times. The doctor is called upon when things are going wrong, to restore or cure from crisis. The farmer has a patch of land and plants, and has the task of maximising resource in terms of desired output. The fisher, by contrast, has time to contemplate, to cast a line in one direction or another, to act on hunch and intuition. It is the art of fishing which most needs to be cultivated in the training of managers and for which management training is least well equipped (see Figure 1).

We can use and abuse the images in different ways. In teaching pupils to manage their future, what is the balance between the skills of train-driving, farming, doctoring, and fishing which the teacher should be promoting? In the running of a school, as of any other organisation, what is the balance and progression of the four for teachers? It would be very easy to caricature the classroom teacher

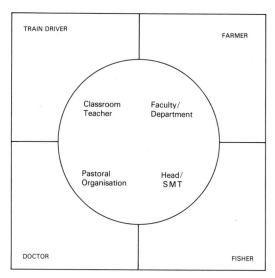

Figure 1 *Involvement in dimensions of management*

as the train-driver, the head of department as the farmer, the pastoral side as the doctor, and the head or senior management team as the fisher. If on the other hand we want for our pupils and for the human race generally some balance of competencies and opportunity across the four, it would be very strange to harden the people in a school organisation into different functional levels. Whatever the hierarchies imposed by past practice or present politics, there is an overriding concern that all educators should in some measure share in the whole range of management activity. And the more we explore the four images themselves, the clearer it will become that there is much more potential for change and improvement to the whole of a society if the train-driver also fishes, or the doctor also farms. Even more fundamental to the health of an organisation is how the four activities work together and interact.

The alternative of making distinctions between those who are most capable of one or other function, and training them for that and that alone, has been tried and tried again in human history and found wanting. I hope, but do not know, that de Bono was not looking for the super-breed of managers as fishers. If he was, he would not be without company in the schools. There was a time when the 'Master' was the qualified teacher and the assistants unqualified; the Arnoldian image dates from the same era. There remains a collective notion of 'staff', both sub-professional in management terms and exclusive in relation to those outside the system. There have still been heads in comprehensive schools who have claimed that their job is to have nothing to do, that they are the people who do the reading and thinking. *Ten Good Schools* (DES, 1977) has been quoted and

requoted for years as showing how important the head is and, therefore, the salary differential. There is still the assumption of something
akin to Jansenist efficacious grace, and all the isolation that goes
with it, in the appointment of heads and in the attitudes of those
who work with them. *L'école, c'est moi*, 'my school', 'ultimate
responsibility', all are still with us. Hierarchy and collegiality are
constantly at play. We are by no means 'beyond domination' (White,
1983). So what legitimate response do we have to a government
department in which the dominant chord is 'we are in control now'?
It is neither to respond in kind, nor to accept rhetoric as fact. The
response has to be one of promoting power-sharing and empowerment, within and around school organisations. The behaviour has to
be consistent with the behaviour we want in the next generation,
and where at all possible in the government of this one. That is what
I mean by educative change.

Forces for change

There are management tools for change which are familiar across all
kinds of organisation, enterprise or service. They are a valuable
part of the equipment of those who manage schools. What is more
fundamental than the management tools, however, is how they are
used. Let us take the example of force field analysis, (see Figures 2a
and 2b), which is perhaps rather more than what Bernard Shaw
would have described as weighing up the pros and cons and then
doing something disastrous about it.

As a management tool, force field analysis is 'neutral'. Its 'political'
position in the spectrum of management approaches very much
depends on how it is used. It may be used privately by an individual
anywhere in an organisation. It may be used privately by an individual with responsibility for the organisation. It may be used by an
activist group or by a senior management team. So it can advance
personal power, or a particular cause, or the 'establishment'. In all
these instances, it can be seen to be a tool of manipulation. It
excludes, disenfranchises and relegates the excluded to a sub-professional, indeed sub-human status, as inanimate objects to be subjected to physical forces. It is non-educative, and indeed runs counter
to the educative management process which I am suggesting is necessary in schools if they are to match in their organisation what they
are promoting in their study programmes. Force field analysis used
in this way can also be self-defeating. It assumes latent conflict. It
only takes two potentially opposing wills to apply the same technique
in opposite directions to raise conflict to the surface.

What happens, however, when it is applied openly by a group
which represents all the different approaches, who recognise their

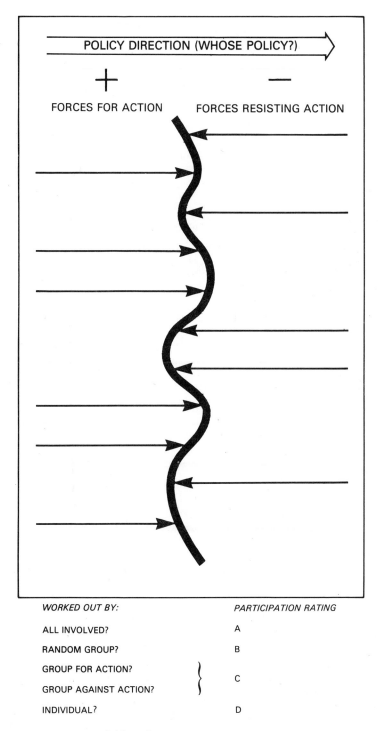

Figure 2a *Force field analysis*

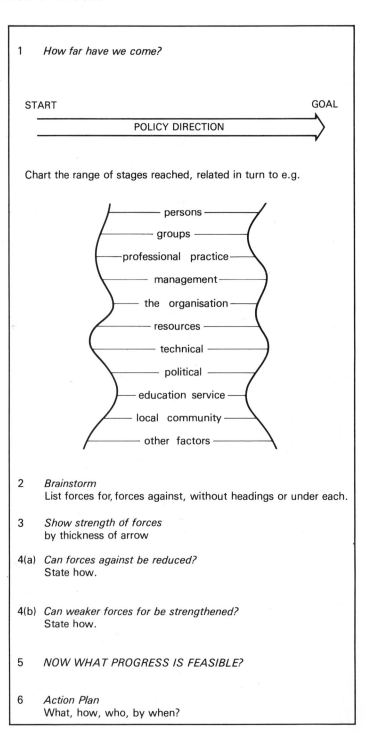

Figure 2b *A procedure for working on force field analysis*

differences, and who start with an agreed overriding purpose to find ways forward together? It then ceases to be manipulative, or a tool by which minorities or individuals either reinforce power or seek to extend it. If all relevant members of an organisation are involved, working on themselves as well as each other in a corporate transaction, it ceases to be about mechanistic forces and becomes organic and educative. It is about regeneration and organisational self-development.

Two examples may illustrate the point, one from within a school framework, the other across schools in a service. A school is still divided about mixed-ability groupings. The theoretical advantages are recognised. The research which points to some advantage in practice is accepted. Everyone agrees that it is a good thing in principle; but some teachers are apprehensive about changing their own teaching practice and acknowledge that their limitations are a barrier to desirable change. Others point to the lack of appropriate resources and training. In such a situation, it is perfectly reasonable and possible to analyse the situation together, openly and with mutual understanding, to tease out together what the real obstacles are, to work on strengthening forces and resources conducive to desirable change and modifying those which are hindrances. This is particularly likely to be productive if people work together on setting time-spans for change. Given three or four years, people who recognise the need for change but fear they cannot cope with it are able to be party to a self-preparation plan; given until next September, their apprehension will be uppermost and the project may run into such resistance that it has to be shelved. However as soon as they are party to a commitment to prepared change, they may well find it can be implemented earlier than at first envisaged.

A second example may relate to falling rolls and surplus places. Everyone can see that there is one school too many. Everyone would like their school to survive. Everyone can understand that others have the same feelings. One argument might be to ask them all to accept a decision made by a neutral administrator, perhaps an education officer, and agree to do what they are told, provided they can see the system operating fairly. But there are all kinds of weakness in this approach. Schools and officers are not isolated either from each other or from the political or neighbourhood communities which they serve. Nobody can be really neutral in a human social situation. If moves are made without being felt to be right, they will generate resistance and counter-moves anyway. If transactions are kept private, they will be met by demands for public enquiry as a means to block proposals. It is politically unattractive to force through a school closure against the will of voting teachers and parents. So why not have the whole thing out in the open, as a part of an educative community's decision-making right along the line? If the facts are incontrovertible, there is the task for everyone of coming to terms with them; if they are not, there is no sense in keeping the issues under wraps just for fear of losing control or having what seemed to be a single direction of desired change made more complex by the range of different insights. If it is more complex than at first appeared, so be it. That is not an argument against action; it may require different management tools.

FOUR

Managing the Community Dimension

School management is no longer about ships and captains on the bridge. It is about managing the currents and seas which are part of everyone's life and learning. Social change affects both the practice and the theory of management. The changes around schools are themselves part of a whole shift in society: there have been uneven changes in the context of community; the structure of the education service has altered; there have been massive changes in the whole environment of learning; there is a new and less desirable continuity from schooling to youth training and prospects of unemployment; and the new laws of the 1980s have had at the same time a controlling and a destabilising effect largely unrelated to changes in the context of young people's lives.

A century of schooling

In the first half of the twentieth century, far from belonging to the local community, secondary schools were about protecting able young people from local limitation; the privilege of segregation would lead to professional opportunities elsewhere. Elementary schools, meanwhile, remained the business of local towns and parishes, in which most young people would remain. It was mass warfare, not mass education, which disturbed that.

A major effect of the 1944 Education Act was to separate the whole of the secondary age population from neighbourhood continuity with primary schools. Schools were expected to contribute to the physical, intellectual and spiritual development of the community. Reorganisation to comprehensive secondary schooling reduced the divisions within the age group, but in Britain did little to restore the continuity of schooling across age sectors which had been broken by the advance towards secondary education for all. By the creation of larger schools in the causes of programme viability and economy of scale, comprehensive reorganisation required larger schools in order to bring the benefits of a wider range of opportunity to all; and the large school also offered less generous local authorities the prospects of economies of scale. In many areas it increased even further the physical distance between secondary schools and local communities. Improved road transport stretched the possible distances even further, and small unviable rural community schools were closed through the 1960s and 1970s.

Despite the immediate post-war mood of social reconstruction, and the desire for coherent reform across social, educational and other related services for a welfare society, public services remained separate both within central government and within local authorities; indeed they were drawn apart in different tiers of local authority, regional or national structures, funded from separate sources, organisationally prevented from working together. Housing, health, education, social services, probation services, and employment policies have remained separate. The principles of corporate management were confined in the 1970s to each separate tier of local government, without bringing them together. It remains difficult to bridge across inadequate systems in developing cooperation between schools and other services related to the same children, families and communities.

However, there have been good examples of community development promoted through the education service. The rural village colleges developed by Morris, and still associated with Cambridgeshire, have been repeated in several parts of the country. The Leicestershire community college continues to develop despite recent threats, and there have been attempts to create all-purpose education centres in other localities, notably in the new towns. Elsewhere, a variety of youth or adult wings are to be found in most areas. Access to premises and facilities and dual use of adult and youth activities are attractive politically, despite the practical economic, organisational and professional difficulties which arise if these are merely 'additional extras' rather than part and parcel of the system. Where the effort has been made to extend the concept of the school or college as a community resource, the varieties of community school practice are as numerous as are the definitions of community education. The differences which may arise from the distinctive needs of each community are one thing; but most of the differences which exist result from inadequacies in concept, system, professional and political will. In some urban areas, the school system is not seen to be capable of developing a community service, and the higher level of alienation and truancy from the formal school system leads to less permanent alternative centres, often in the run-down premises left from school closure. Voluntary associations, some of them attached to other large institutions such as churches, temples or mosques, may or may not work with the schools service. Sports associations are more usually in communication with lower tiers of local government than those which have the school sports fields and sports halls, and it takes much to bridge the divide. The difficulty is sometimes compounded by separate leisure and recreation bureaucracies in local government, and this could be increased in local authorities which try to avoid the radical effects of local management of schools by passing the premises to other services with schools seen as one user among others. In large-scale new town projects, there are examples of an overall community development programme to which energies and services can be harnessed.

More recently, the practice of individual school governing bodies has been extended. These are a channel for community involvement in the school, and for the school, including its community representatives, to reflect and project back towards key interest groups in the area. The governing body has its origins in the voluntary foundations on to which a maintained system was grafted. Required by the 1944 Act, it was in some areas no more than a token body, sometimes the education sub-committee under another name and across a whole group of schools, although in other parts it was the body to which heads felt responsible. From the early 1970s, it became politically dominated by the now politicised local authorities, and was widely held to be technically a sub-committee of the council, its legal status still being a matter of doubt. Since 1980, it has begun to respond to the calls for power-sharing across local interest groups; in the 1990s, the intention appears to be for it also to have a direct line from central government, whilst serving as the consumer interest with a direct line to parents as shareholders. The trend towards governing bodies as partners in decision making about the curriculum has been made less significant by the Government's intention to dictate curriculum anyway. Governing bodies are still not being seen as the vehicles for a community's involvement in planning and developing the contribution schools make to the community's learning. They are a formal channel for home-school groups, which have developed in a variety of forms, and which remain free of legislation to grow into more active forms of local partnership.

Issues of corporate control

In the history of the education system through the last one hundred and twenty years, 1870, 1902 and 1988 are the most obvious examples of central government take-over; balancing these, there have been releases of control which have been used to reassert local educational initiative. The Redcliffe-Maud Commission on local government (1969) had two main planks for reform. Local authorities must on the one hand be viable for their largest responsibility, statutory education; and on the other, new boundaries must reflect the areas to which people relate, by settlement, shopping, work, and culture. The first criterion, which was the more suspect, was adopted; the second was the victim of electoral pressures, and the recommended boundaries were altered to preserve political advantage. Some local education authorities felt like a community; but many were not. Worse, the two tiers of local government separated education and social services from other community interests; in the shires, housing and recreation and leisure were part of another tier of local government altogether – the district councils. Police services meanwhile became regionalised; medical services have their own national structure with lines to regions, areas and districts not necessarily related to local government. This continues to be a hindrance to cooperative modes of community management.

Corporate management has also suffered from being misused following the Bains Report (1972) and its adoption in local government reorganisation in the early 1970s. The principle of corporate management is in itself excellent. A council organises its committees and executives to set priorities across the whole of its resources and responsibilities; but when corporate management is applied to an incomplete local system, it makes it more difficult for any one service to relate to others which are not part of the same authority. And where the local authority is not felt to be really local at all, the transactions of corporate management are divorced from the clients and delivery points of each service. In a local community, services which are each tied to background detailed planning and decision making are less able to work together than before.

The politicisation of all local authorities has had a different effect; political parties already determined the way councils ran in larger urban areas, but before the 1970s it was possible for the shires at least to be run by 'independent' councillors; it was possible for the education service to be detached from political pressures on other services; and it was usual for governing bodies to be 'above' politics, or politically unimportant, depending on one's perspective. By the mid-1970s, that had all changed. Local authorities, education committees and governing bodies were all politicised. That is the context in which the Taylor Report (1977) attempted to restore a significant role and a balance of interests on governing bodies; the 1986 Act, together with the local financial management clauses of 1988 has largely put the Taylor recommendations into effect; but the context of government intervention has meanwhile changed.

In the education service, misapplied corporate management had two significant effects. First, education officers, like their counterparts in social services and others, were drawn into a senior management team with the chief executive, and thereby drawn apart from the specifically educational activity of advisers or from the local schools and services. Secondly, heads, schools and governing bodies were isolated from corporate policy and planning and found it increasingly difficult to identify with authorities which were less local and whose principal transactions were not specifically for education. This alienation has been reflected in surveys of heads in particular; and it has caused constant conflict and stress within local education authority departments. The conflicts inherent in the shifts of management structure were made much more acute by the mixture of reductions in central government finance, falling rolls and school reorganisation and closure. It is against that background that schools are being tempted to 'opt out' of concerted local planning altogether, to cultivate their own local clientèle with central government backing.

The more sensible reaction has been to move towards local financial management for individual schools and colleges, first by local authorities piloting their own schemes, and then by government legislation. For internal school management this can be turned to advantage, and a later chapter explores the opportunities more fully; but in management terms schools are not necessarily each the cost centre for all activities to which they contribute; and community education is about cooperative contribution across the schools and services within reach of a locality. Corporate activity in a really local community has yet to find effective forms of management.

In the last decade, the already weak foundations of a partnership service, on which community education is particularly dependent, have been undermined. Isolated from each other and starved of resources, local schools and services became dependent on direct central government interventions and initiatives, first through arms of government which were able to bypass education service procedures – the Manpower Services Commission (or Training Agency) of the Department of Employment and also the Department of Trade and Industry – and then through the Department of Education and Science, taking control of specific priority funding areas.

Curriculum and community

Many of those now leading and governing British secondary schools have been inspired by the ideal of a 'total education' provided by an enriched and extended form of schooling to educate the 'whole person'. That is the approach inherited both from the times when elementary schools were the main source of knowledge for the masses and also from the privileged social refuge of boarding schools. It was reflected in the design of earlier comprehensive schools with their 'house' structures for personal and social interaction, and with their separate pastoral care patterns of staffing. It was reflected too in some approaches to community school development; as much as possible of the education provided for a local community should be channelled through the school, with the emphasis on access. Perversely, it is wrongly assumed or implied in curriculum literature and in the 1988 Education Reform Act that the taught and timetabled school programme is the whole curriculum and should correspondingly represent balance and breadth, without reference to contributions to learning from other sources. Schools are then held accountable for the overall standard of educational achievement, and this is measured by school assessment and terminal school examinations.

These assumptions are in different ways convenient both to teachers and to those who are critical of schools, but we are all aware that the social and technological changes of the last one hundred years, and in particular of the last twenty years, have given young and old alike access to other learning experiences which are at least as powerful as those provided by schools. What has sometimes been missing is the recognition of real or potential learning in everyday experience, in the home, in the workplace, through increased mobility and through new media and access to information beyond what an institution or its staff can provide, however well endowed.

Once schools and provided services are seen as part of the whole resource available to a local community, their management requires a total reorientation of thinking and organisation. They may be seen to complement rather than comprehend learning opportunities; to compensate for lack of opportunity and specific deficiencies in an area; to coordinate and take into account learning resource whether within the school or beyond it; to collaborate with each other and with other services. Schools are then part of a radically different notion of 'comprehensive' education, in which breadth and balance are life-wide and lifelong, not school-bound. Once people have new access to information and instruction from other sources, teachers have more of a role related to learning skills which can be applied out of the school orbit as well as inside, to social interaction, to counselling, to group learning, and to work requiring hands-on experience of particular specialised equipment. None of these has much to do with the traditional base of the 'classroom'.

The continuum of learning

Not until arguments for dividing people into distinct categories at the age of eleven were shown to be ill-founded, and comprehensive schooling had extended from primary to secondary education, did it became possible to recognise that continuity was at least as important as a distinctive environment. After the Plowden Report it became permissible from 1967 to organise schools across different age spans, including institutions to provide for the middle years of schooling;

the way was open to compare and contrast the experience of young people in primary and secondary schools, to examine the continuum of school process and content. The need for continuity of method, content, ethos and personal relationship has been most acutely felt by those meeting special educational needs; and because of their different history in the medical services until the 1970s, many special schools have been protected from the division between primary and secondary stages.

However constricting the terms of the imposed 'national curriculum' may be, it can be modified eventually to provide a coherent view of learning between the ages of five and sixteen. It remains a problem in Britain that comprehensive community education is still envisaged and usually organised in age sectors. The severance is artificial, and an essential component in managing either primary or secondary schools in context must be to provide a system for bridging between the two, with a strong foundation on both sides of the divide. It is no foundation for lifelong learning to keep the two apart. In management terms, the bridging should extend across professional relationships, curricular programming, sharing information on and access to skills and resources, identifying long-term trends and needs for the neighbourhood, knowing how each other's school systems work, cooperating on all aspects of pupil transfer including record systems, providing continuity of access and involvement for parents, and where appropriate making joint appointments for specialist skills, including the specialism of transfer across the middle years. These are all basic elements of a cross-institutional management structure required for effectiveness. So the transfer role of the tutor is particularly important, and requires time, focus and skills beyond the internal programme of the school. Open enrolment and the 'choice' across different kinds of school make continuity more difficult to achieve; but continuity ought to become the selling point to reduce the problem.

The same principles apply across secondary, youth, adult further and higher education. It is no longer thought that secondary schools would merely combine the functions of elementary schooling for the masses to engage in paid employment, and preparation of a small minority for extending their initial education at colleges and universities. Changes in patterns and availability of employment and also the recent habits of some politicians and industrialists to use secondary schools as the scapegoat for the political, social and economic problems of national decline, have brought with them programmes of full-time and part-time further education and training programmes which in many parts of the country are more significant than direct entry to employment or transfer to higher education put together. They lock places of work into a compact of shared responsibility for education and training, and even a compact of employment in some recent schemes. The two leaving and continuing functions are still recognised and combined in the secondary schools examining systems of GCSE and GCE A level. But the new and much more significant titles are TVEI, YTS, CPVE, and BTEC. The first of these, moreover, has had the most marked effect on patterns of continuing professional development for teachers. So the school-work interface has to be regarded in a very different way. From being the somewhat unlikely scapegoat for industry's difficulties, schools now form part of a new continuum, in an educative partnership with others and subject to the same kind of scrutiny. They are also themselves significant and sizeable centres of employment.

Turning the new ERA

The Education Reform Act appears to be contrary to much which we are identifying as needed for the future. Rather than cooperation in contributing to the local community, it relies on market forces and competition between institutions. It espouses a basis of school curriculum which appears to be entire in itself. It encourages even more testing for purposes which have still to be satisfactorily established. It appears, by encouraging schools to 'opt out' to undermine a capacity for local policy and planning. It takes further the process of central controls rather than local interpretation of needs. It inhibits initiatives. It limits the role of the teacher rather than extending it outwards. There are, however, one or two details of the new legislation which can be used to help move towards meeting future needs. Local management of schools, including local financial management may appear to limit the community aspects of schooling by confining responsibility to each separate school; but if local policies for financial control include encouragement to manage community education, and given criteria which take account of local needs, local management of schools could be turned to advantage, especially if clusters of schools and services use their powers to combine resources.

Through governors, local financial management and more involvement in staffing decisions can be made to express real involvement in practical policy direction by representatives of the local community. The governing body may have been conceived by those who steered through the 1986 and 1988 Acts more as a vehicle for accountability than as a channel for the views and aspirations of the neighbourhood; but it can be developed in that direction and become a model for involvement, rather than being just a board of directors to whom teachers become partly accountable. As the Taylor Committee recognised eleven years earlier, that kind of structured involvement can represent one of the most significant elements of adult education yet seen in Britain. The new governing bodies will have to find the balance between caring for their particular school and working with other institutions to provide a better service than any one of them could offer; between projecting the school's purposes and reflecting the perceived needs of local people. It will, at best, represent a balance of interests in formulating policy about what is taught and how, who is to teach it, what is to be the ethos and culture of the school, encouraging and supporting worthwhile developments, acknowledging achievements, bringing different experience to bear on the way a school works and is seen to work.

Managing community education and recent laws

Whatever the form taken by community education, it has to measure up to five criteria, They are access, involvement, shared governance, use of the community as a learning resource, and a relationship with lifelong learning. In other public services, despite the doubt about their survival, there have been significant moves towards a community development model. In the health service, a community approach to promoting health and reducing or preventing the need for institutionalisation has been positively promoted by government. The care of the mentally infirm has taken on an open community aspect. Community policing has returned. In the prison service, institutionalisation has been questioned and community rehabilitation emphasised. In education, however, the only element of recent legislation which was consistent with such general trends has been the 1981 Education Act for Special Educational Needs; but that has been variously implemented and the aims of integration are likely to be undermined by the 1988 Act.

The 1988 Education Reform Act removes the word 'community', as used in 1944, from its statement of aims, preferring the similarly undefined 'society'. Where it is used, the word 'community' appears to be more than anything else the business community. Ministerial responses show that drafting civil servants have community use of school buildings in mind, but little else. The circular setting out guidelines for local financial management does offer a definition, but it is not one which we are likely to take seriously. The community school is blandly, and with doubtful logic, defined as one in which there are non-school activities under the management of the school.

In terms of access, the 1988 Act does not register the trends of needs, demands or likely patterns of society in the near future. The demands include equal opportunity and parity of esteem for a much wider spectrum of negotiated learning, crossing the formal labels of what the 1988 Act conceives as 'curriculum', crossing general and vocational learning, across modes of learning, and crossing age groups. That requires a managed system of opportunity, flexibly responsive rather than bureaucratically directed, related to a shared policy framework of social renewal and reconstruction. It will need a very different framework of laws.

Management has also to be adapted to the criterion of involvement. It is not just 'extra-mural' activities which are going to use school facilities, or schools and pupils who are going to use something out there called the community as a resource for learning; they are a part of that actively educative community which will be sharing in identifying and developing its resources, including the professional skills and the physical resource of teachers and schools. There will be other kinds of contribution from other parts of a community if it really shares responsibility for education. There will then have to be a new partnership in planning and organising the way learning is negotiated.

Partnership also presents problems of definition. It is one thing to subscribe to principles of partnership in learning, involving learners and teachers and, certainly in the case of young people, their parents. What is less easy to define is responsibility for making the partnership work. It has to be shared; but if sharing is to work, the apportioning of responsibility has to be defined and agreed, and there has to be some mechanism for doing that. We are probably talking of an active form of corporate management within a community to which people belong and subscribe. To make full use of each other in an educative community, there has to be a constant review of the actual and potential partners and contributors. Management will be in structured teams within organisations and by structured teams across organisations. Managing teams across organisational cultures and managing organisations as part of a cross-organisational whole-community approach becomes a key responsibility. Management across organisations must affect the ways in which responsibility is to be developed.

What is now needed is a new approach to distributing responsibility in a contributory society changed and informed by the revolution in communications technology. The management roles may still be of the kind identified and recognised anywhere, within the different categories identified by different observers. But it is no good defining these within single static organisations. In a federal task culture, with constant re-grouping to complete newly negotiated projects, those roles may have to be undertaken by different people in each situation. Community leadership is about engaging all those people in managing shared values across systems and structures. The networks for planning, resourcing, delivering, controlling and reviewing education will depend on a form of leadership which has to do with seeking consensus in value systems, involvement in strategic thinking and planning, and commitment to a constant of change to make sense of changing situations.

Such questions have an immediate bearing on issues which over the last decade have predominated in planning school provision. The 1944 Education Act placed a clear responsibility on local authorities to provide for school education appropriate to age, ability and aptitude, and on the parents to secure such an education at school or otherwise. The decision about the appropriateness of school provision lay in the first place with the local authority, subject to rare and usually vain appeals to central government or recourse to law. The position is now more obscure. Is a society to plan to provide what has been identified locally, through local government and professional advice, to be appropriate education within a broad framework of national law, or is it the mission of national government to provide a choice, through which parents can determine what they consider is appropriate? If the latter, it is arguable that direct state intervention is appropriate in encouraging, setting up and funding alternative schools. Should a society create space for schooling which reflects individual parental views on gender, race, social mix or creed, even if that undermines an overriding policy affecting all parents and children or the future well-being of society as a whole? Should it condone or encourage the purchase of privilege if that is the way parents with money choose to spend it? Or should it apply a school policy of bringing the young together as a means of building a more cohesive society or of levelling up to equal opportunities? No government and no electorate can have it both ways.

There appears to be a view in government which is alternatively centralistic and anarchistic: central government will determine in detail what should be taught and examined in schools in the public service; but every encouragement should be given for either schools or individual parents to opt out of that service, and to exercise collective and individual parental choice even if that disrupts the planning of educational provision for the local community, or is socially divisive. It is legitimate to seek some alternative rationale which might have more hope of accommodating different views across our tense society.

The chimera of choice

A school system should encompass an element of choice, not be disrupted by it. As in any part of a democratic process, individual choice can be promoted, but not at the expense of others' rights. There may be a case for choice of schools equally esteemed, equally resourced and equally effective in what all schools are expected to do in general as well as what they have to offer by way of distinctive qualities or programmes. That is a far cry from the purchase of real or assumed privilege which must by definition be to the real or assumed disadvantage of others. Some of the larger schools with distinctive house or hall sub-communities have been able to offer internal choice of environment. The reasons for choice may be highly personal: there are very powerful factors which defy reason. These have to be taken more seriously than rational analysis of matching school programmes and policies to individual needs. They have to be anticipated in the ways schools and homes communicate. But these are choices which can and should be accommodated within a policy of providing for all according to real learning needs.

More important than institutional choice, however, is the choice of what is to be learned. Education has been seen as promoting individual autonomy. That involves young people in decision making within the school process. Again, the question is how far to involve parents with them? Because of the individual focus, the question has often been posed as an alternative. The process of decision making is more likely to be productive if it is a shared and cooperative process across young people, teachers and parents. If that is more of a problem during adolescence, it has to be worked on rather than used as a reason not to do so. The young person's right of freedom from the pressure of parents is in itself no prescription for lifelong learning. It has to be translated into negotiation on equal terms towards positive outcomes.

Internal choice may be offered within a predetermined programme or the choice may extend to sharing in determining what the programme and what the choices should be. It is one thing to make arrangements to ensure that an attractive choice of educational fare exists; that is just artful shopkeeping. It is quite another process to involve those with an interest and possible contribution in thinking through what choices are for and developing what the offer should be. There is no justification for either a secret garden of curriculum development or for a government to attempt to prescribe the curriculum to teachers, parents and young people alike. Equally, there is no justification for teachers or parents to accept either of these uncritically.

Choice in education is not so much about choosing which school as about identifying which resource, school or non-school, is best suited to any one learning activity. Such decisions on the use of alternative resources and instruments for learning depend on those trained to teach the young in classrooms becoming community-oriented educators and negotiators, promoting and responsive to the involvement of parents with their children in a responsibility being worked out together.

Current legislation and the way it is enacted may be sending out contradictory messages. Within the political span of the last decade, we have seen the 1980 Education Act, which in its own way promoted public and prospective parental access to information, and sought to increase parental choice to select schools still within the priority a planned local framework of provision for all. The 1981 Education Act appeared to reflect one of the Warnock Committee's strands of thinking, a cooperative partnership of parental and inter-professional response to needs; but in its regulations and their implementation in local authorities, it shifted back to relayed stages of a statementing process in which the decisions are taken neither by parents nor by schools. The 1986 Education Act is more clearly tinged with the consumerist approach and with choice in the market economy rather than public authority as the ultimate sanction for accountability to the shareholders. It does, however, create opportunities for real parental and other local involvement in the governance of schools. Finally, the 1988 Education Reform Act appears to take back most of the ultimate decision making to the public authority, this time the central government of the State; parents, governors and local authorities are relegated to being the watchdogs of the State to ensure that schools do what they are told. School governing bodies appear to have greater control over spending, staffing, sanctions and curricular decisions, but only as a means towards ends dictated to it. Both choice and involvement become State-directed activities, if that interpretation becomes accepted. There is, moreover, the encouragement for parents to exercise a collective choice rather than an individual one, to have the school nationalised in a 'grant-maintained' status more distanced from local decisions. The powers of parents collectively as shareholders emerge more strongly than the individual parental rights and responsibilities with which the new prescriptions are being sold.

The recent legislation hardly touches that community context of learning; rather, it conveys a notion of accountability to provide a commodity to the customer. Yet the pattern of developing partnerships is more significant than the more limited functions of representation and accountability which may have been uppermost in the minds of legislators. If education is about learning relationships, it is more important for teachers, parents and young people to work together than for each to have their say about how the others are doing. The confidence to review and be reviewed by each other can best develop from cooperative decision making. It is not just a matter of three parties supporting and commenting on each other's work; within that framework, young people can support and resource each other, parents can help each other, and teachers, so often isolated from each other, should be able to develop in teams. This will only work if schools are organised to make it work. For a variety of reasons, schools have now to be so organised. These partnerships are the most likely productive ones for the future. They cannot be left as optional extras. They have to be fostered to the full meaning of partnership, with all the shared sense of purpose, the mutual respect and the real dialogue between parents, pupils and professionals which can be a basis for continued negotiated learning beyond school.

Developing school management for community education

Current legislation is there to be turned to good effect, and then if necessary, to be reformed. Management processes have to be made compatible with the immediate changes which are being made for schools, and then we have to go beyond these changes. Local management of schools is just one example which may be turned to different effects. To respond to real learning needs, the way ahead is to go beyond the transfer of responsibility to institutions, and to enable each unit of resource to work through networks, partnerships, matrices of the kind which may also be the way forward for group learning processes; through inter-dependence rather than independence.

Who is in the groups? Local management of schools gives the opportunity to identify the many tasks which teachers are carrying out and which could be better done by those trained for them – the clerical, administrative, technical, bursarial, and estate management tasks, possibly the public relations tasks, too. The management of the physical environment of learning and the effective administration and communications of any organisation have to be related constantly to values, mission, aims. Local management of schools is not about more administration in schools; it is an opportunity to extend

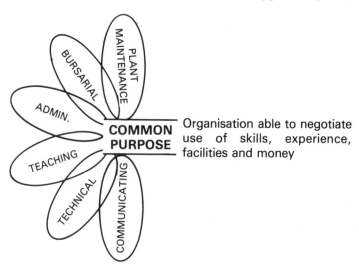

Figure 3 *Common purpose for all parts of the organisation*

and develop the management responsibilities of non-teaching colleagues in the organisation and beyond it (see Figure 3).

If that is how local management works, then clusters and consortia
will not be just recommending without resource, but will be empowered to put their acts together there and then. That goes far beyond
problem solving in particular instances; consortia have to agree such
priorities as positive action to address the particular needs of a
locality, so that there is common purpose within and across organisations.

We shall have to ask in management terms whether the school or
college is the management unit for all or most purposes. Indeed, the
only definition we seem to have of a school is that it has in all cases
a head and, by now, a governing body. Local management may be
about an organisation for 200 pupils or 2,000. Institutional viability
depends, moreover, on the service to be provided.

Devolution of financial management to the institution is only a
starting point, not a replacement for a proactive and responsive
local service. Self-reliance or autonomy is a starting point for active
partnership, not a replacement for inter-dependence. Responsibility
for resources involves a responsibility to share them to make best
sense in a locality. A starting point in a local group is that any aspect
of management priorities, even including admissions and public
relations, should be addressed in collaboration with other schools,
further education, youth and community services and neighbouring
secondary schools as a joint resource to a local community. The
second stage is to extend the decision making to other services and
to share in theirs. We do not have to mind each other's business all
the time; but we may well have to identify different people and
resources across organisations, to take on a particular role to meet
particular needs; and to do that, we have to have an organisation
not above but across organisations working in concert (see Figure
4).

Future strategies must also relate to the likely opening effects of
new technologies. The management of the school organisation and
of learning through it will, in any case, be changed radically by
computer-assisted administration and by computer-assisted learning.
But managers of schools have now to contemplate the future in which
information will be more accessible at home than in school, when
networking across a community becomes as significant as the classroom once was, when open learning systems move from open university to open college and polytechnic to open school. Whatever we
have initiated and developed in schools has to be related to the new
opportunities right through people's life-space and lifetime? And if
schools become not the repositories of knowledge and learning, but
key contributors to making the most of learning experiences out
there, that must affect the way schools are organised, and the nature

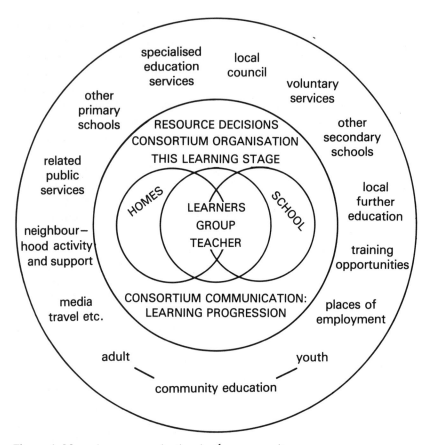

Figure 4 *Managing communication in the community*

of leadership. The leadership required for the future is educative leadership in the community, and community education is the context for all future teachers. For that to be more than rhetoric, communications have to be managed.

The continuum of management

Over the last few years, first heads and then heads and deputies have been pulled apart from other teachers. The issue is not just whether teaching is more important than managing the organisation; rather, it is whether there is to be a continuum of management responsibility involving all teachers in what has been called a 'covenant of leadership' (John, 1980). On that depends how we are to envisage management development policies. Refer back to the concept of the teacher as a manager of the learning process. Now the learning process is not just to do with formal learning programmes; even that part of curriculum which is school-engendered encompasses what HMI described as 'the climate of relationships, attitudes, styles of behaviour and the general quality of life established in the school as a whole' (DES, 1981).

The agenda for school management training suggested by the Department of Education and Science is seriously restricted in three senses. First, it appears to be for heads and senior staff only, and therefore to consolidate a particular way of managing schools. Secondly, it is unrelated to management training for other branches in the education service, or for governors. Thirdly, the priorities seem to be about effective execution of predetermined policy, not for its planning and development.

So the Department of Education and Science adopts a 'task force' of industrialists and educationalists who are intended to advise on training heads and senior staff in schools for local financial management, national curriculum and other legislated initiatives. That is not developing management. It would doubtless affect the operational, and perhaps touch the tactical; but it does not appear to relate to strategic policy formulation in schools. Fortunately, the worthwhile consultancy groups brought in have been correcting that tunnel vision too.

Management development for future contexts includes all teachers' preparation and development, a much higher priority for skills and attitudes which have to do with the education of the community as a whole and to lifetime as a whole; it is likely to be pointing both towards a collegiate form of school management and one which involves other professional services, parents, and other interest groups in real decision making about education.

That is not a one-way system; educative leadership in the community involves teachers at least equally in real decision making about what happens in the other areas of community development. Management programmes will have to be developing a continuum through the management of learning to the management of teams in an organisation and across organisations. Despite current funding systems, it will be helpful for strategic policy-forming to bring together people from their islands of responsibility to be a resource to each other rather than separating out specific target groups. Priority now has to be given to working across organisational cultures and not be trapped into cultivating just our own patch.

Management for development or for improvement?

The Czechs have a story about *perestroika*. Taken through a Russian-Czech dictionary, it shifts from reforming and re-structuring to a word which means re-establishing what was happening already. Much the same can be said of 'improving quality'. It is essentially static. It demands training which will enable people to do better the things they were doing before. The tactic of throwing money at training for specific national initiatives is inadequate. There is a simple political attraction in targeted priorities for specific changes; but there is a gulf between managing changes and managing change. Put together 'improving quality' and 'priority initiatives' and the system improves its capacity to stand still, while adding bolt-on components which have little effect on the whole existing process or on each other. This steady-state model has been reinforced by funding structures and funding mechanisms of most education services. The mechanisms for looking across or outwards are rarely established. Priorities are usually established through separate institutions and phases, and executed through separate purse-holders. That will not in itself change by transferring the unit of management from a discrete authority-wide cleaning account, for example, to an institutional general account.

Management has to be about sharing vision and turning it to everyone's reality. It is not so much about assimilating and responding to change by executing it effectively. Instead, the priority has to be to enable all who contribute to education to be involved in constant change and development of the whole service, in anticipating and indeed engendering worthwhile change.

Teachers and the management of community education

Teachers will not be based in schools; they will work from them, not just with children but with adults. Work with parents has to become a core component of the professional task. It is now accepted in the initial training of teachers that work with parents and in the social context should be a part of the initial training of every teacher; but most of the teachers who will be in schools for the next twenty years are already there, unaffected by recent changes to initial training. So it is even more important that this priority should be put into in-service training, too. The way teachers' time is organised does not include much more work with parents than required attendance at parents' meetings within directed time. So the management of professional time, location and communication has to be re-designed.

Professional development involves developing the role of the tutor in a community. There is a radical change of expectation and attitude which puts involvement in community development and social skills first, and the specialist contributions second. Those who have responsibility for significant areas of curriculum – for departments, faculties, or cross-curricular teams – have to develop the ability to negotiate school programmes in relation to community needs and alternative resources available. They have an active role in creating access to school programmes, from other age groups and across schools. The cooperative community dimension has to be built in not just to job descriptions but to the way the job is seen and done. Teachers as credible community tutors and curriculum negotiators have to have plenty of community involvement themselves. *Pace* the Department of Trade and Industry, that goes beyond getting some industrial experience or being aware of what is going on locally in the world of work as though schools were not a part of that anyway.

Priorities for training and developing school management teams at all levels must change accordingly. There is an immediate need to work on managing outwards, on negotiation with other schools and services. The grey areas of external management are the ones which heads and teachers feel least confident about and which they least enjoy, because of the ambiguities. This has to be turned into positive navigation and channelled communication policies, involving all teachers and not just the head. It is as important for the head to distribute community responsibility as it is to recognise the greater subject expertise of specialist colleagues. The senior management team has the particular responsibility to develop structured partnerships with other organisations, and to develop the capacities and the organisation of the school accordingly.

That is particularly true of the development of communications policy and practice. Communication cannot be developed only from one side. Communication is about interaction between people; between schools and other centres of employment, schools and parents, schools and other centres providing education; between the 'internal' and the 'external' communication of any organisation or identified group. It is as much about listening as about informing. It may be in developing this area of management that the newly constituted governing body has most to offer, as a meeting place of interest groups. If so, senior management teams must be involved with governors in empowering minority and disadvantaged groups, very often articulate among themselves, to gain access to the communication channels of structures and organisations. Then those communication channels have to be capable of transmitting a very much wider communication policy than either the accountability or the access models have offered. It is through local communication that the values and best practices for education are most likely to be transmitted.

Funding and resourcing professional development has to be managed as flexibly as the intended outcome. There must be scope for virement across the funding for teachers and the funding for governors. There must be agreement across services to fund joint programmes. The issues of community education must be thought through together. Teachers' centres should become public education centres, a source of information and a resource to the whole community, bringing together the professional wardens and those who are creating parents' centres for educational advice and support. They should be easy to reach, welcoming social and training centres for professional and voluntary groups. They could be part of a community school.

Schools and centres should be linked by computer, and have access to national as well as local information. They should provide an adequate general purpose training base for the education service, including ancillary and auxiliary workers based on schools – clerical, administrative, technical, caretaking, grounds maintenance, transport or catering. One key service to introduce, as argued in a later chapter, is to update or re-train those who have been away from teaching and want to return at least to the level of responsibility which was theirs before. The computer together with inter-active video, and doubtless cabled networks in the very near future, will be there as tools for self-education, not only for programme-led groupwork. Information technology should be developed with confidence, to the point where the human resource, the materials, the media and the physical environments of learning can be shaped together.

Management programmes to develop the community dimension of schools will bring together managers from education and other centres of employment, other professionals and elected people with public responsibility training together. From the few examples which have been tried, it is evident that management training programmes for school leaders, advisers and governors together, in-house, across a local community, and across local boundaries, make good sense for a future agenda of shared management of schools in the community. The mode of training and development has to fit the different circumstances of these different groups. Programmes will develop exploring self in relation to others, team-building, managing differences, power sharing, shared governance of schools, assertiveness, managing to influence the decision-making process, shared strategy and development for the organisation, effective use of time, personnel selection, managing resources, communications policy and practice, the continuum of responsibility for education and training across schools, colleges and employment. They will not just be about these matters, but will be a part of bringing people to work together.

In a community dimension of education, the management model is one to which all schools and services will subscribe, which will be client-led and context-embedded. The resulting local forum of organisations, perhaps a community education council, should be adaptable to meet changing needs, which it has to be capable of identifying. It should be able to pool and re-direct resources. It should have a high profile in the community. It must link up statutory services and voluntary groups, across general and vocational, education and training, informal and formal modes of learning. There should be a formal commitment to them, written into the job descriptions and the organisational aims of every part of the services represented. From each school, we should be developing cells of activity, small and personal groups, such as the teacher as group tutor developing small teams of parents around their common concern, parents quietly resourcing each other. The voice of teachers and parents, the shared governance of schools, the articulate educative community, have to grow outwards from such groupings; they will not come from legislation.

FIVE

Management and Teachers

Much is now changing in the school staffroom, not all because of legislation. The 1986 Education Act has established teachers as governors, though unfortunately excluding non-teaching colleagues from the governing body. The 1987 imposed conditions of service for teachers will, in the long-term, have helped define what the teacher's role is and what work should be done by non-teaching ancillaries. The 1988 Education Reform Act has established the power of governors in schools exercising local financial management to 'hire and fire'. The belated realisation in government that a shift of national curriculum has to be matched with teacher supply seems also to be causing a retreat to licensing non-teachers to teach in shortage areas. Mobility across schools and further education sectors is likely to increase. Professional mobility across the European Communities from 1992 will also have effects as yet uncalculated.

The distinctions previously made between the head's role as chief executive in an organisation and as leading professional in a teaching community have felt wrong, at least in the large secondary school. Those of us who moved through the head of department or head of year 'middle management' to deputy headship or headship levels were always conscious that thereafter our teaching was subordinated not only to our other responsibilities, but to the leading professional, the head of department on top of an area of expertise under whom we, as heads and deputies, worked as less and less skilled teachers. The head of department did not have 'delegated' responsibility; even in our own specialist area, it was a responsibility we were quickly disqualified from resuming, and in other areas there was never any question of being able to choose to 'delegate' or not. The situation was one of distributed leadership rather than delegation. It was a collegiate relationship rather than the hierarchy which showed on the constricting two-dimensional staff lists of the organisation.

If that dual notion of headship vested in the same person was ever valid, it will have been eroded further by recent events. The notion of the head as leading professional has obscured the responsibility of professional leadership. Organising and enabling the collective of colleagues to help pupils learn will always be a prime responsibility. That responsibility, unlike the leading professional one, is not transferred totally to particular specialists, even if there is a focus in someone else's work as professional tutor or INSET co-ordinator. Professional leadership and responsibility for the professional nurture and development of the whole human resource of an organisation is shared in some measure by heads, deputies and heads of faculty, department and year. It is inseparable from the responsibility for acquiring, distributing and maintaining resources in general which, because it was couched in resource language, was wrongly distinguished from the professional role. Professional leadership extends from an element of partnership in teachers' initial training; to appointments, whether of teachers or of non-teaching colleagues; to induction into first posts or new roles or a new school; to promoting and helping to provide in-service education and training, not least in a school-focused mode; to matching people's skills and intended tasks; and to the whole range of relationships in the common room, in the governing body and in the community.

It is not only the head who is now being edged towards the management role of employer, previously scrupulously avoided in principle if not always in practice. Teacher-governors may now be directly involved in decisions on the appointment of the head and deputies, and they are part of the complex of influence and support in the staffroom. Staff redeployment procedures, first voluntary and then compulsory, have eventually required the head to nominate those to be redeployed. Local management of schools not only brings with it the power of governors, including the staff governors and probably the head, to require the local authority to dismiss staff; it also brings the power of the whole staff to be engaged in choosing within the school budget between human and non-human resources. The employer-cum-employee relationship is brought into the staffroom.

For those new to it, local financial management may at first seem to isolate schools and their groups of teachers from each other as though they were units of management in every circumstance, which of course they cannot be, however large the schools or however well run. Eventually, LMS should increase the capacity of schools to work together on the sharing and development of resources, not least of people. There are several areas for immediate improvement in the way people work across institutions in any one locality. One is in the field of meeting special educational needs, where the Grampian 'wedge', the Banbury 'sector' (Sayer, 1983) or the ILEA 'cluster' (Fish, 1985) of organisations has still to be developed more widely. Secondly, it is still possible for heads in an area to work together to encourage shared staffing, transfer or exchange, to anticipate and prevent the fears and formalities of redeployment procedures, and the delay and uncertainty which they can cause to staff management as a whole. Thirdly, it is more important than ever before to give concerted attention to the disadvantaged position of part-time teachers, many of them women, who have been all but excluded from local authority promotion and in-service development opportunities. Local financial management can put that right, but only if schools work at it together in a locality. Fourthly, much the same has to be said about the supply teacher, by now the most sought after commodity in many areas. It ought to be possible in future for schools to build much supply cover into their staffing establishment, having anticipated the general level of absence through ill-health and out-of-school professional activity including INSET. There will still be a case for sharing some supply staffing locally. And there is a very strong need indeed for supply teachers, however employed, to have access to professional development from which they have been excluded. Fifthly, there is good cause for schools in a locality to combine to give training opportunities to groups of people who are isolated in any one school. These may be teachers of minority subjects. They are even more likely to be non-teachers: the welfare assistants, caretakers, secretaries, and workshop or laboratory technicians, for whom recent legislation has done nothing. Finally, in any one community, there is a strong case for shared work across schools in the training and development of governors, who will also need to see each school in the context of the total educative resource to that community, and be given a perspective beyond the competitive market economy one to which they appear to have been introduced. These are not matters which can be dealt with under separate categories of management. They are at the same time led by curriculum or educational need, they are a part of professional development, and they have to do with the management of the most important and expensive resources in and across organisations.

Staff appointments

Procedures have previously varied according to each local authority's guidelines and according to the wishes of each governing body; but whatever the procedures, the head and deputies have a central role in the appointment of colleagues to the school, and this will in future be shared, even where it has not been shared previously, with governors, including staff and parent governors. Procedures have become more standardised, and more consistently school-centred. But local authorities and recent legislation have become more prescriptive in order to honour commitments to existing teachers at a time of falling or fluctuating rolls and in order to conform to recently imposed conditions of service. The timing and relationship between redeployment procedures and school appointments under the local management of schools has still to be worked out and modified. On the other hand, local financial management points towards greater flexibility in the choices to be made. There may well be local policies of positive action to balance the teaching community; with or without these, each school has its own adjustments to make to achieve a balance of age, gender and ethnic background, in appointments and in promotion.

The actual process of teaching and non-teaching appointments is as good an indicator as any of the real staff relationships in the school, whatever may be the rhetoric. It is too often described and indeed treated only as personnel selection. That indeed is the brief given to researchers by the Department of Education and Science. Yet an appointment is at least as much a matter of school and career selection by individuals. Again, it is too often seen as a matter of finding a round peg to fit in a round hole. It could equally be an opportunity for the hole, or perhaps the whole, to adjust and adapt to a changed set of relationships, as a part of the professional development of those there already and not just of an incoming colleague. If the development of teaching and learning groups through teams is to be undertaken seriously, there is a strong case for identifying how people are likely to work in a group. It is curious that the insights of social and industrial psychology are so seldom applied to school appointments. Some such 'light' instruments as the Belbin diagnosis could be applied, but if a diagnostic procedure is applied only to

Figure 5 *Building the team*

assess a person to be selected, and not equally for the incoming person to assess those already there, it becomes a one-sided selection again. Mutuality of professional assessment and appraisal starts here.

Induction

Initial training, especially the brief post-graduate year, cannot prepare adequately for particular school situations; so all who are new to the teaching profession require a training programme in their first year. As far as possible, such a programme should be for all newcomers, whether experienced or not. It is also a time quietly to make sure that those new to teaching have made adequate arrangements to be fed and watered, and know how to survive without salary for the first month of contractual barbarity.

Many schools have formally delegated responsibility for the work of incoming teachers, to team leaders or mentors to introduce them to their new tasks and environment. In addition, it is recognised as good practice to vest in a professional tutor or equivalent the responsibility to provide an induction programme of value to any newcomer at whatever level, and to be readily available, supplementing rather than replacing the responsibility of subject or pastoral team leaders. The professional tutor will be in a less judgmental position towards the newcomer, and have more of a judgmental role in commenting on how the school is managing the induction process.

An induction programme has to be costed out and built in. It will probably be most systematically structured in the first term, and will include formal and informal arrangements for teachers to discuss their work with those to whom they are responsible, and with each other. It will include opportunities to study the context of staff responsibilities as a whole, from the practical 'where to go for what' to some appreciation of what others are trying to do. It will cover the local arrangements for communications, contacts with parents, assessment routines and documentation. It will give opportunities to discuss problems as they arise. It will enable incoming teachers to take a full and immediate share in decision making affecting all parts of school life. There may or may not be an LEA input for incoming teachers. If there is, it should be incorporated in the school programme. The head will wish to have informal and probably formal discussion with each incoming teacher in the first half of the year.

Probationary periods of employment and teachers' entry grade requirements with national or LEA guidelines should be fitted naturally into such a programme. Formal mid-year appraisal for new teachers will now be more healthily related to the school's general appraisal scheme, rather than appearing to be exceptional. But it will still be the first time, and important in developing future habits. It has to be an open transaction, and not come out of the blue. A new teacher must be able to recognise that those responsible know and have seen what they are talking about. That will have been most easily managed if cooperative teaching and comparing notes are customary; the formal solemn visit to the back of the classroom is just not good enough. Mid-year review should not be only about initial 'performance'; it is also an opportunity to review the job as it has turned out, to modify it for the following year, to share perceptions, and to establish the mutuality of appraisal which has to go across the whole school if appraisal is to escape from reinforcing hierarchy.

Once in a while, however careful the selection and induction of new teachers may have been, there will be a serious problem of mismatch where the new teacher is not coping or contributing adequately. It is part of the job of headship to face that kind of decision and make sure it is being faced by the teacher concerned. It should also be shared, so that the resource of the local authority, perhaps the original training institution and certainly those who can help in the school are brought together in solving the problem, without shame or self-flagellation. It is necessary to have professional advice when making decisions which will affect someone's whole future and livelihood.

In-service education and training (INSET)

Writing from within the system, we are all still part of the 1960s, in which professional development, organisational development and curricular development were part and parcel of each other and of the professional-political-popular consensus of the most liberated period in British education; of the 1970s, chasing government to do something about the James Committee (DES, 1972) and its own promises, and chasing our tails in schools to promote professional tutoring and the thinking school, despite the siege mentality of cuts in population, spending power and political priority; of the early 1980s, in which the last surviving representative and consensual quango in the national education system – the Advisory Committee on the Supply and Education of Teachers – put down markers for initial and in-service education together, (ACSET 1982, 1984) and was promptly put on ice for its services, with its recommendations moulded to serve a very different imposed political direction.

The James Committee became part of the professional parlance, and some of its recommendations were willed to happen or even believed to have come about without actual change of system or provision. The government white paper: *Education: a framework for expansion* (DES, 1972) proposed that long-term release for INSET should amount to three per cent of teacher salary costs. In the wake of the Great Debate, this target was actually put into financial estimates for 1979, but was suspended by the incoming government led by the original Secretary of State who had supported the proposal. It remained the basis for such publications as the ACSTT document which a group of us wrote to be circulated by the Department of Education and Science to all schools in the late 1970s, *Making Inset Work* (DES, 1978) and for the Department's publications of the early 1980s (DES, 1982, 1983). The recommendations of ACSET (1984) were based on a figure of five per cent, which in some of our calculations was thought to have corresponded with the James Committee's recommendation of three per cent for long courses alone.

INSET should always have been the priority. Even in times of less rapid change, there was no prospect that initial training could equip a teacher for a whole career, or that professional growth could just be left to happen. But in a period of falling rolls, with the struggle to retain what has already been achieved, with the relative immobility and lack of career prospect for teachers, INSET becomes more obviously important, both to counter stagnation and to reduce the lead time between the need for change and the capacity of the service to transform itself. The expertise of teachers is no longer to be seen as one of knowledge or even of the skills to impart it. The credibility of teachers as organisers of learning experiences depends on their perceived ability to organise their own learning and practise what they promote.

The 1986 change to a more sharply defined scheme of grant-related in-service training (GRIST) mixed a selection from the recommendations of ACSET and from the mechanisms of TVEI-related in-service training through a separate government department. The further step of channelling national training priorities through local education authority training grants (LEATG) has done much to improve effectiveness, but little to provide a coherent pattern of professional development which would offer a broad range of opportunities to teachers whatever their particular school or local authority situation; teachers, governors, parents and politicians have still to recognise the paramount importance of in-service development, to share that awareness, and to develop a school organisation which will enable teachers to benefit from continuing professional education without it being felt as a disloyal interruption to their main tasks with pupils. Early school identification of training needs, modular timetabling and in-built supply teaching together could provide solutions. And if only schools could move more rapidly to the modular courses being proposed, there would be opportunities to build modules of INSET into timetabling, in such a way that it ceases to be an interruption of teaching programmes. That would also help provide training opportunities at times when access is most feasible (see Figure 6).

Example: 50% of teachers' programme includes:
1 INSET module out of 12
Planned 1 year in advance of key stage
Additional staffing built in, not 'supply'.

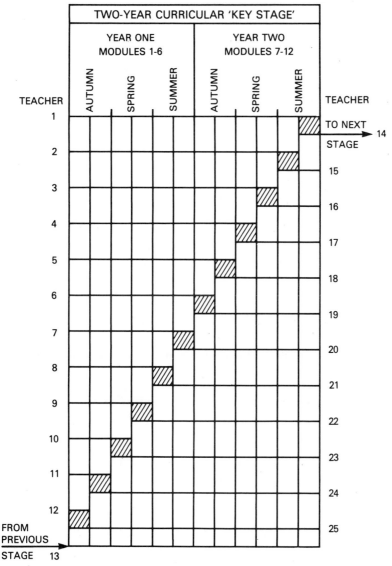

Professional and curriculum development needs identified and negotiated in advance with LEA and training institutions.

Training programmes timed to fit modular curriculum.

Teams across schools by negotiation.

Figure 6 *Modular curriculum and professional development*

Another part of the solution will come through careful use of the five days earmarked in recent conditions of service, and at present used extremely well by a minority of schools, and very badly by a minority of others. There will be some further scope for schools to build INSET into their organisation through local financial management, particularly where local authorities have distributed a significant element of the protected INSET budget directly to schools.

The GRIST scheme and its later modification is now under the rhetoric of progress actually reducing the range and depth of in-service experience (Sayer, in Clough 1989). It also remains conceptually flawed, although the parallel movement towards institutional self-evaluation may provide a partial cure. Largely because of funding mechanisms, INSET has too often been conceived as the additional opportunities specifically provided under separately categorised, organised and funded activity. It then becomes associated with courses out of context. For some teachers, it is associated with additional qualification as a step to promotion; and that is the perception of other teachers who do not take part and comment sourly on those who do. Many teachers, including those who resent an overlay of INSET which disrupts their prime purpose of teaching pupils, are also annoyed by national or local encouragement to take part in INSET programmes which are inadequately funded or avoid having to provide for replacement staffing.

Development through learning is central to the purposes for which schools exist; and that approach must include the development of teachers. In everything that teachers do in school, there is a potential element of professional development. Every decision about who does what is also about a professional learning opportunity or about reliance on proven experience. That, as an attitude to staff development, is more likely to make best sense of added INSET opportunities than the concentration on becoming proficient in delivering government-funded priorities. Within the current system of LEA budgets and LEATG submissions, the school has to identify and agree needs and priorities well in advance, through its development planning. If INSET is to be built into the annual organisation and not to be seen as a last-minute intrusion on scheduled and planned activity, a formal three-year cycle of planning will make sense, as recommended by the Audit Commission for local authority budgeting. A rolling programme will include a systematic annual review by each colleague and by each working group in the school, of what has been found valuable in the past year's INSET; what is the involvement in the current year; and what are the priorities for the near future. These views can best be sought in a standard formulation, which may well be incorporated in staff appraisal procedures. INSET planning must relate closely to staff development and appraisal as a whole. A draft programme of INSET can be drawn up for agreement among the staff and negotiation with the LEA where additional resources are required; and it can be negotiated with INSET agencies beyond the school where it is considered that provision can best be made with their involvement, or by them alone. At the same time, the school can use the individual staff returns to prompt further discussion or to communicate what planned INSET provision in the future is most likely to meet expressed needs.

Group needs and priorities related to those of the whole school and to development projects across schools will lead to longer in-service courses involving secondment, provided the identification of needs is related to strategic planning and not confined to knee-jerk responses to shifts of political funding tactics. Longer secondments have been lost to the profession in recent years; when the balance is restored, they must be planned, managed and pursued by the whole organisation. A school which plans to make use of the training, experience and insights gained during a period of secondment, and to use the work done is also likely to use the secondment of one teacher to provide different learning experiences for others, with something of a planned domino effect. What appears to be a single secondment may actually contribute more to volume training and organisational development than will several short courses for a large number. INSET planning has to start from planning what to do with the experience, the effects and the intended products of INSET.

Managing the staffroom

The management of a staffroom is essentially a matter of relation-ships and people, not closely aligned with the structures of staff responsibility, and in many ways more complex, more three-dimen-sional, for the staffroom is not just a professional workplace. Indeed, few staffrooms are in that sense professional at all. Does the staff-room include a professional library? Is it usable for professional meetings? Perhaps more significant is the general feeling of being at ease there. Is it felt to be equally accessible by men and women? Has it developed clique areas? In some schools, the head is a visitor in the eyes of colleagues, in others an intruder, in other unquestionably a member. What does it feel like to a newly appointed colleague, or to those visiting for interview? Non-teaching staff of all classifi-cations, or language assistants, students engaged in teaching practice, visiting professionals may be welcomed and made to feel they belong; or they may be stranded and uncertain of the house rules. There are varying receptions at the door for visiting parents and voluntary helpers, or pupils with enquiries? What does the staffroom feel like to a governor? What does it feel like to the families of staff members? These questions mean a great deal to teachers and non-teachers alike.

Yet the staffroom does not figure on most management courses, and until recently (Hargreaves, 1984) very little developed thought has been given to what it is, whose it is, and what it does to people. In a school where the continuum of management responsibility among all colleagues has meaning, it is particularly important that the staffroom should reflect the intentions of the whole place, even if that includes having places to let off steam. So it would be rather curious if the whole staff were not involved in determining the management of their common ground.

Some pointers for the future

Any large organisation or significant service has to find a shared vision of what is wanted and what can be achieved. To do that, it must share as accurate a prediction as possible about the way life and learning will look later, whatever we do about it. Some of the likely changes have been referred to in other chapters. Perhaps the most significant one for schools is that the curriculum in any real sense cannot be confined to the school contribution. Once upon a time it may have seemed that way, whether in the 1988 Act or in the mediaeval cloister or in the parish schools of the nineteenth century; school was where you went to get your learning. Travel, postage, telephone communication, newspapers and books for the millions; then radio, gramophone, television, video and information technology have changed all that whilst we continue to legislate ludicrously for a complete curriculum in school subjects. The school medium may still account for about one-third of learning for the young – for some, much less, for others more. The rest they share with all ages, at home and at leisure. Even knowledge, skills and understanding of the sciences, which might be expected to depend on school specialists and laboratories, are now being shown to have come more from learning outside school than inside. All kinds of learning opportunities are now accessible through the new media, with which, on the whole, homes are better equipped than schools, and in which the young are generally more competent than their teachers. Distance learning controlled by individuals is making inroads into the former preserves of institutions like schools. The new media add to the variety and informality of learning.

Does that point to de-schooling? That will depend on schools and teachers being able to identify their role as coordinators of learning experiences not just in classrooms but in the curriculum of life. It will depend on filling the gaps which schools can best fill; and that cannot be done without first identifying and then identifying with the whole community context of learning experience and opportunity or lack of it. That involves the teacher and the school in issues related to a multiracial and multicultural society, not least its potential for learning and new insights. It involves them in the whole range of social backgrounds and learning attitudes and needs, including those currently perceived as special (Sayer and Jones, 1985). It involves them in making connections with what learning is going on in the different parts of young people's lives. In the previous chapter, therefore, I have suggested that the prime role for the teacher of the future is community education and the coordination of learning wherever it is happening. That is most likely to be developed through an extended tutorial role as the core activity around which a school organisation is formed (Sayer, 1987), in which the teacher is helping to identify what learning is happening, is negotiating what learning can best follow, and is pulling together the skills and resources most likely to be useful from within and beyond school.

That is a management role from the start, requiring a repertoire of communication skills and powers of organisation. It is likely to become crucial as schools face outwards. There is still a place for specialised resources which people come to because the resources cannot so easily come to the people; and there is an important place for social interaction and meeting places for learning in which people can share each other's resources.

Classroom control is still seen as the most critical factor in the success or failure of the new teacher (DES, 1988). There is a real problem here, for the classroom is becoming less and less useful for learning, and may be expected to become less central to the way schools are run. Disciplined processes of group interaction are therefore going to be more important for learning than classroom control, however necessary that may be as a starting point. Subject specialism will also have a different kind of importance. When information can most easily and most accurately be obtained through access to the new media, the teacher's knowledge of a subject and subject teaching methodology is more important as a motivator and source of confidence than as a source of knowledge. The sight of someone enjoying continued learning and knowing and showing how to go about it is more important than a pretence that teachers know all the answers, with all the disillusionment that follows the discovery that they cannot. Schools should be about organising the shared pursuit of learning.

People are likely to learn how to work in teams by working in teams; and to be helped to work in teams by people who work in teams. They way schools work and the way people work together to make them work is the first perception young people have of social organisation. So school management is a key area of learning, not because anyone wills it to be but because it is there. Political and moral issues are exposed in the way adults work together in the school community, and in their openness or resistance to children's participation in school decision making. That is just one more reason why recent legislation could set schools back, by debarring pupils from school governance, unless schools find their own equivalent ways of involving pupils in real decisions. Schools which hold a mirror to society have also to be working out and trying out better ways for society to function. Teachers are involved in using the school organisation as a learning experience for others as well as themselves.

As the trained expert in pulling together and helping make sense of learning, the professional teacher needs to know how learning happens. A psychology of learning applied to school systems (Jones and Sayer, 1988) and a repertoire of learning methodology are part of the professional equipment for all teachers, not just a few on the margins. As an essential part of the management of learning, skills of assessment and evaluation have to be highly developed not by an expert minority but in all teams of teachers. It may be that when the current obsession with the testing of pupils as a means of controlling teachers has been cured, schools may be left with the more valuable by-product of skills of assessment and evaluation developed not by 'experts' but in all groups of teachers as essential tools in the management of learning.

The future for teacher education

The ACSET criteria for initial teacher education, which were adapted as the criteria by which the government-nominated Council for the Accreditation of Teacher Education (CATE) was required to scrutinise training courses, reflected an uneasy compromise between two conflicting views. Through the early 1980s there was a constant battle between the perceptions of those now in government who were looking for a return to enhanced subject specialism and specificity, and those of us who were looking for flexibility and openness to the constant change which we saw as the future of schooling. That conflict is now taken into the national curriculum.

Initial education for teaching and in-service professional development must together promote what teaching is likely to be about and what an educative society wants for its future. Subject disciplines and subject teaching classroom methodology have dominated people's perceptions in pre-service education, on the terms in which teachers are appointed, on the timetabled habits of school operations, and therefore on initial training. Certainly there must be opportunity for curricular renewal; the teacher's enthusiasms and demonstrable talents as an inspiration and example of continuing learning must always be there, if we are to avoid the current danger of merely carrying out government-controlled programmes as functionary technicians. But what teachers will not previously have experienced is the whole context in any pupil's life of their own specialist contributions, and it is the context which must be worked upon as the priority of in-service education, even more because of the continuing subject dominance of initial courses.

Cross-curricular development in teams is needed so that all teachers as tutors have a grasp of the whole curricular offering of the organisation in which they work; and the priorities are not those of the national curriculum in the 1988 Act; they are about relationships, group skills, communication and negotiation beyond the school, organisational insights, open shared management, access to the new media and social contexts which make up the curriculum of lives as they are being lived.

Teachers must work together with those who will guide learning in later phases, and those who have guided earlier, so that curriculum is seen as a development through life, not just as a diet for the school day. Schools have to be organised so that teachers are brought together with the other parts of an educative community: governors, parents, community relations groups, media, other services and professions, to make joint decisions on how best to resource across the whole context of a young person's present and future learning experience. That cooperative resource approach will probably best be systematically developed by a local representative community education council. A later chapter registers the particular priority for the inclusion of peripatetic, part-time, supply and potentially returning teachers in local plans for teacher education.

Schools and the other services round them have to be organised to enable that kind of shared learning to happen without being felt to interrupt planned programmes. A modular school day and year in the curricular organisation should include modules for teacher education, programmed in as part of the school's learning, and therefore not interrupting anything or anyone else. Higher education training centres should also adapt their programmes to a compatible modular arrangement, so that there is access to their modules from the school organisation, and so that they can make consultants available for modules to work in schools.

For that to work, the programmes of in-service education and the learning opportunities included must be the result of a three-year planning cycle of negotiation, implementation, and review, related to school review and professional appraisal cycles. Training events and consultancy episodes can then be planned as part and parcel of professional development and school and service review. Such modular arrangements should encompass both pre-service and in-service teacher education. In order to secure access to teachers wherever they are working, the teacher-training functions of higher education must become part of a regional planning consortium, bringing together the needs of local communities and the resources within reach of them.

There must be some means of making professional and planning sense of regional and local systems for teacher education. There exists at the time of writing a complete vacuum; the Government has been so obsessed with taking control that it has neither restored ACSET nor set up its own appointed body to replace it along the lines of its curriculum and examination councils. The best thing that could happen for the education service in the early 1990s would be the establishment of a General Teaching Council (UCET, 1988), representing together the professional insights of all sectors and regions, the organisational insights of local and central government, and the partnership insights of parents, governors and employment. This key proposal is developed further elsewhere in this book.

In the short term, the emphasis for government-funded INSET may well be on specific targeting for particular and discrete priority areas; on controlled 'licensing' to develop programmes or to take on responsibilities; on blanket exposure to recognisable training events; on strengthened subject expertise. That is a fact to be lived with rather than a direction to be followed. Indeed, it provides yet another reason to emphasise the crossing of boundaries, the contextual, the cooperative, the process-oriented and learner-centred modes of development which have been outlined here for the new situations in which schools and teachers, along with others, contribute to the curriculum of lifelong and lifewide learning.

Staff appraisal and organisational review

Any apprehensions about formal appraisal schemes introduced by statute are unlikely to be about having appraisal itself, but about what will be the actual procedures, about alterations to them being imposed, and about this being yet another uncharted pressure on time. Another doubt about formal appraisal schemes is that they may be ineffectual rituals, as they have been in other sectors of the public service. Schools cannot afford to waste time on mere formalities. Teachers were asking for formal appraisal and promotion schemes long before the Government showed any interest.

Moves towards accountability and towards formal review procedures must in the long term result in a greater emphasis on conditions of service, beyond those now imposed, and to the inclusion within them of activities which are still expected yet unquantified, or voluntary and beyond the call of individual duty though expected of a good school. Schools have not run on contractual obligation, which has been minimal, but on professional expectation, goodwill and trust. That will remain true, provided that employing authorities and government come to realise that without planned resourcing they will no longer be able to expect much which has previously just happened in schools. Intended activity has to be reflected in the budgets delegated to schools.

Staff review procedure affects the ethos of a school and its external and internal relationships. It affects professional collegiality and organisational hierarchy. It may change the position of the head and deputies. It may be inflexibly applied and receive inflexibility in response. It has a bearing on the relationship of staffing to other resources in new financial management contexts. It could well push the local advisory service into a second-tier inspectorial role. All this is true; but it is equally true of an absence of such procedures.

Staff roles and organisational structures have both to reflect long-term aims and to be adapted to changing circumstances. Professional review has wider implications than individual development or performance, particularly in terms of staff relationships and of power. A serious danger for heads is that formal schemes of appraisal, coupled with apparent increase of powers over resources, may appear to increase the head's power over colleagues, and thereby reduce the scope for their professionality. That is not what most heads want, but it is what others most fear. It is also the most likely short-term effect; democracy takes time, and nationally legislated schemes have to be assimilated. A collegiate approach to responsibility and decision making inside the school may be damaged by inappropriate styles of appraisal. Beyond the school organisation, appraisal and organisational review will change the nature of partnership and cooperation between heads, local authority officers and advisers; unless the changes are identified and understood, professional relationships may be damaged. The task is to avoid both those dangers, and to discover and develop the strengths of new legislation. Whatever the reservations, any head must now be prepared and competent to manage a system of formal staff appraisal, must be able to minimise the dangers and to draw on the advantages which some schools have been able to see.

The appropriate model for staff appraisal in schools and the education service is not line management of individuals, but group openness and mutuality. Staff review is not just the business of the head. There is a test here for the ethos of the school community as a whole, to engage in open mutual and positive appraisal across and beyond the multi-faceted tasks of teachers, and to relate perceptions of individuals to the development of the organisation as a whole. It would be odd, in a school organised for teamwork, if appraisal were to be solely about individual performance or need.

The values reflected in schemes of professional appraisal have to be the same as those which determine approaches to school self-evaluation and organisational development. Within the school, as many people as possible should be drawn into contributing to assessment of the whole organisation and its parts. Schools exist as partners in a service and with other schools, despite being set at odds with each other. Governors and parents have a valuable part to play in the review of a service for which they are responsible or on which they depend. The perceptions of pupils are the keenest of all. If their judgments are uninformed, open discussion in a strong tutorial system is the way to develop them. Mutual appraisal is going to happen anyway.

No review can properly be made of a school in isolation from the rest of the local authority. Organisational review schemes should involve those who work in schools in reviewing education departments and sections, just as they should involve advisers in reviewing schools. Properly applied, such cross-referencing may not only improve awareness of priority needs for planning purposes, but have the makings of a professional approach to an education service viewed as a whole.

Activity-led staffing

The staffing of schools has been determined largely by custom and practice. The pupil-teacher ratio has no basis in pedagogy; its authority may have derived from the Talmud, from the size of classroom constructions, or from the maximum numbers of children to control. More recently, it has been determined by local authority budget norms. The monitor system and methods of Bell and Lancaster in the early nineteenth century at least derived from a theory of learning, an ethic of sharing knowledge, and a realistic approach to the size of learning groups.

From the mid-1970s, positive action to reduce disadvantaged groups led to staffing formulae beyond the basic classroom ratio. It can be seen at work in the area of special education, from 1973, in the attempts to identify language and cultural enrichment needs for commonwealth immigrants in the Home Office Section 11 schemes, and in the social indicators of needs which led to such innovations as the London additional use of resources scheme, which was also the first significant pilot scheme for local financial management.

Approaches to curriculum-led staffing in the early 1980s were prompted largely by the concern to protect a necessary range of formal subjects during a period of falling rolls in secondary schools. The number of teaching groups rather than the number of pupils became the basis of teacher numbers. Curriculum-led staffing policies were often accompanied by positive action to reduce social, educational or organisational disadvantage.

By 1983, the Secondary Heads Association was moving towards

what it described as 'task-related' staffing proposals, which took account not only of the numbers of pupils, the number of groups, and the special factors affecting the delivery of a curriculum, but also the time needed for other expected tasks, including those which make school organisations work. These proposals were fed into the new Audit Commission, which came out the following year with its very similar proposals for 'activity-led' staffing. There was some reflection of this work in the Government's 1987 conditions of service document. Some local authorities began to move to a 'curriculum and organisation' model of staffing.

In the post-1988 financial delegation to schools, each local authority has been trying to translate whatever stage it had reached into the formula for the school budget, simply in order to give individual schools a measure of continuity from which to deviate in a planned way.

The recent change to formal job descriptions linked to contractual conditions of service established by statute underwrites the head's task to identify for governors what time and whose time is needed to complete tasks not confined to the pupils' timetable. Time for staff appraisal has been mentioned, and for that there there are a variety of initial estimates appearing within the framework of 1265 hours each year; appraisal schemes require resourcing by the Government for its imposed will, if they are not to be at the expense of some other activity. But the conditions of service as they now exist are no more than a start. They leave as voluntary activity or as undefined reasonable expectation much of the work without which schools would become unrecognisably restricted and probably unmanageable. So much has been added to the expected tasks for the secondary school in the last two decades, both by teachers themselves and more recently against the will of the teaching profession, that the whole framework of school organisation needs recasting, first to accord with what actually happens, and then to match society's intentions, when these can be identified. We are much closer to a system which requires resourcing to be part of society's will; and at the same time schools are now able to determine what human and material resources are most needed in their particular circumstances.

The combination of staff appraisal and local management of schools is bound to bring about further changes. What do teachers actually do, and how is their time intended to be spent? As long ago as 1977, research into what teachers actually did showed that whereas schools are staffed and organised as though only 20 per cent of a teacher's time were spent on professional activity beyond the classroom, (and in primary schools as though the classroom were the whole story) the reality was that classroom contact took only 21 per cent of professional time, with preparation, administration, negotiation, training and other invisible overheads taking the other 79.

By now, the added pressures of external liaison, of one-to-one trans-actions with young people and their families, of regular and detailed assessment of pupils' progress and achievement, not least in recent changes of public examination, of accountability and communi-cation, of planned response to ever more rapid social and technologi-cal change, of professional collaboration and interchange, will have widened the gap between reality and the myths on which are built the teacher's assumed school day and year. Part of the staff review exercise must be devoted to identifying more rigorously how time is spent, how it can best be saved, and how it should be budgeted. That exercise must in turn inform the employing authority, whoever that may be in future, and must be the starting point for negotiation on overall funding and resource levels.

In community schools, the disparity has already become obvious: there, the 'school day' is blown wide open, and it is no longer possible for people to pretend they perceive the school as nothing but the formal subject timetable for pupils. It is now the governing body of each school which will determine the nature of the school day. Three-session days, flexi-time, and modular approaches to the curriculum may not be the immediate effect of financial delegation and certainly not of nationally prescribed curriculum and assessment; but once the initial adjustments have been made, it is these organisational developments which will be seen as the longer-term opportunities of the next decade.

It will no longer be accepted as good management to describe as extra-curricular and to therefore make no allowance for those many activities which are part of a school's intention for pupils' learning experience, and part of its 'contract' with parents and the community. If they are not built into time provided, they will not happen. That is not to say that teachers will never again give of their free time; but their giving must in future be over the top of the expectations, and given in the confidence that it will not be abused. In the short term, working out a new and flexible resource model may be extremely hazardous and frustrating. In the long term, it will restore health to the service.

SIX

School Financial Responsibility

Introduction

Management of resources has been traditionally considered apart from curriculum management or educational leadership. The separation has shown in the nature of roles in schools, colleges and universities, and also in local and central government departments. It has been held that the skills required are specialised and different. Management of resources will be part of the 'chief executive' function, and probably delegated; educational decision making on curriculum and methodology are part of a professional leadership. This argument can be shown to be flawed in relation to staff development; curriculum and teaching method are inseparable from teachers; teachers are the main human resource and the main cost of a school; their activities depend on an equation with material resource and non-teaching human resource. The argument is flawed in relation to the external management of schools. And it is deeply damaging in relation to management of the physical environment of learning and to financial management.

The physical environment of learning is part of the curricular experience of all who work in schools. It either reflects or detracts from educational intentions. It is a major resource for learning, both in its contribution to the overt curriculum and from its influence in its own right. Much of the subject matter of the subject timetable will have been forgotten; but the exits and entrances, the buildings, the corridors, the playgrounds, the cloakrooms and the assembly halls are likely to remain as lifelong memories. Part of the hidden curriculum, very keenly experienced by young people, is how resources are regarded and used; what priority is given to which activity. If examinations sweep aside all other activity – halls, gymnasia, specialist workshops and laboratories – then they must be more important than the activities they displace. If more is spent on some activities than on others, the same conclusions are quickly drawn.

The schizophrenia between educational and administrative functions in the education service has prevented communication between the two: educators have lacked the information or the negotiating and persuasion skills to convince the public and its representatives of either the priority of education or the educational priorities within its service. If values are to inform value for money, those whose professional responsibility it is to represent educational values have to be equipped to communicate and interpret in the language of resource management.

That is not a responsibility to be left until teachers occupy hinge positions like headship, or become education officers. From the moment they start teaching, they are the major resource for education, using other resources, and drawing on the learning resources of children and parents. Part of the teaching responsibility is to control and harness all potential resources towards the achievement of educational aims.

This chapter is focused on one aspect of resource management, namely financial delegation to schools which may serve to illustrate an attitude to resource management in general. In Britain, local financial management for schools has suffered from too many slogans and misconceptions. One misconception is that the idea is new; another that it is politically right wing; a third that it is about giving power to heads and principals; yet another is that it means more time spent on finance in schools. The evidence of the last half century leads to none of these conclusions.

What is meant by local financial management?

LFM will typically make overt and direct the school's control of a large proportion of the budget allocated to it from all sources. In recognisable pilot schemes, there have been different meanings and emphases. By school may be meant the governing body with recommendations from the head; or it may be the head on behalf of the governing body, and in consultation with colleagues in the school. By control is meant both the responsibility for spending and accounting, and the power to determine levels of expenditure under each heading, viring or transferring funds across budget headings according to the school's priorities. Powers may involve full or partial virement; full or partial control of the use of premises, including control of charges for lettings; carrying forward an element of underspending or overspending into the next financial year.

Local pilot schemes

Items included, wholly or in part, in pilot LFM schemes may have been any of:

consumables: books, stationery, materials;
furniture and fittings: new purchase, replacement and repair;
examination fees: for internal and external candidates;
travel and associated expenses for staff;
unofficial funds;
income from lettings and activities;
communications: printing, postage, telephone charges;
energy: heating and lighting;
staffing: teaching and non-teaching establishment and supply;
appointment expenses;
cleaning;
minor building repairs;
removal of temporary buildings; closure and disposal of surplus
    premises.

More usually excluded have been:

local taxation and debt charges;
pensions, sickness and maternity benefits;
major building repairs and external maintenance;
health and safety at work expenses; pupil transport.

These so-called pilot schemes have in fact been local initiatives
unrelated to likely or intended national legislation; usually, a small
group of schools has piloted a scheme which could then be adopted
across a whole locality. There has been no piloting for the national
scheme now being introduced. There may be some limited transfer
of experience and attitude; but the nature of the legislated change is
of a different order, and the 'pilot' schemes can now be seen in a
historical perspective, rather than as a planned preparation. That
perspective is important, politically and professionally, and will be
pursued later. However, the 'pilot' or fore-runner schemes were not
on the same scale as the national scheme introduced through the
1988 Education Reform Act. On the other hand, some of them have
also been directly related to educational values, to positive action, to
environmental education through energy conservation.

The Education Reform Act: local management of schools

The Education Reform Act requires local authorities to submit
schemes for approval by the Department of Education and Science,
which will in effect locate in the governing body of the school itself
perhaps 90 per cent of the financial management of all secondary
schools and primary schools with more than two hundred pupils.
The schemes will include a formula for funding all schools in which

at least 75 per cent of the total is allocated according to age-weighted pupil numbers.

The immediate questions are not about the principle of delegation but about the criteria and practical implications. The criteria are important, because if they are wrong – and I believe they are – they may endanger the pursuit of a principle of management which is essentially right. The first thing wrong is that nobody, including those who have framed the regulations, can predict what the effects will be in any one situation. Kaleidoscopic management is not the best way to ensure that children will be well provided for. The figure of 90 per cent (later to become 93 per cent if the current intention is pursued) is to mean 90 per cent of the whole general schools budget, including such 'protected' items as specific government funding for Education Support grants, LEA Training grants, Section 11 Home Office grants, Urban Aid, Travellers' children grants, and TVEI. The total for each of these depends on annual bids and allocations. So the figure of 90 per cent is somewhat unpredictable, as are LEA tactics to circumvent the Act.

More fundamentally, the current criteria within the LMS scheme itself limit the local authority's ability to take positive action to anticipate or to mitigate against social and educational disadvantage. It will therefore have different effects according to the levels and range of deprivation within each authority and within each school. That could cause conflict between the educational principle of identifying and responding to needs and the allocation of resources. If it does, the needs simply will not be met. There is very little flexibility in the system, so it depends on the initial criteria for resource allocation being right. In a local authority in which, to quote one example, 40 per cent of pupils have difficulty with English, 40 per cent of families are without a wage-earner, two-thirds of the children have free school meals, and a large proportion have special educational needs, the same criteria for funding will not have the same effect as in an area in which these background circumstances are almost unknown. The principle of providing for a continuum of need has been lost.

There may be ways in which local authorities can compensate for this weakness by the nature of their bids for specific central funding. They may try to weight their proposals for TVEI, for teacher-training, for curriculum development, or for multicultural education towards the activities most likely to suffer from a simplistic approach to the rest of the schools' budget. Central government, in deciding on allocations, will have no ability to relate decisions to the effects of LMS; indeed, there is no ability to relate each specific fund to the next. So the principle of local management is not being applied to these funds, and there will be a lot of confusion in the first few years. The regulations will have to be changed; there are no real pilot schemes through which to adjudge how they should be changed without initial damage to the population and system as a whole. It would be a pity if the damage which will be caused were to lead to a reaction against the principle of delegation itself, which is not only sound in management terms but has a broadly based background.

In this chapter, I want to trace sources of LFM as experienced inside the education service and profession, as opposed to the more recent mythology; to relate these moves to general trends in management practice; and to point forward to some of the positive outcomes which might be anticipated in Britain. Here are just a few of the individual elements which appear to have influenced current attitudes and practices; most of them have been part of the experience of those now running British schools.

The last half century

Secondary schools in the United Kingdom have traditionally had a large measure of responsibility for the way they use their resources: in particular for the use of staff time and the spending of money on books and resource materials. Before 1944 secondary education was confined to a small minority, and much of the 'free place' or 'scholarship' provision paid for by local authorities was in quasi-independent foundations with their own financial management. Maintained schools were not by any means without financial responsibility. In many local authorities until local government reorganisation in the early 1970s, each secondary school governing body prepared its own financial estimates; indeed, the 1944 Education Act's model articles of government indicated a large measure of financial responsibility for each school governing body. Until the 1970s, there was no great difference in the awareness or control of finance and resources across maintained and private schooling; the job of running the school was noticeably similar. The recommendations annexed to the Report of the Royal Commission on Local Government in England, which worked between 1966 and 1969, look very much like the financial powers recommended by the Taylor Committee in 1977. These are now being restored to some and spread to all governing bodies under the 1986 Education Act, and are likely to be extended in secondary schools, further education colleges and larger primary schools in the 1988 legislation.

1 Thwarted 1944 intentions

Secondary schools, in the pre–1944 sense, handled or determined much of their spending and some of their income. This was much less true of elementary schools, and despite the model articles of government for secondary schools in the 1944 Act, local authority administrations did not generally extend to all secondary schools those habits which had been associated with much pre-war secondary education. In 1944, the Command Document 6523 from the former Board of Education had this to say:

> The practice will no doubt generally obtain by which governors prepare estimates covering a suitable period and submit them to the Local Education Authority. Within the broad headings of the approved estimate the governors should have latitude to exercise reasonable discretion . . .

This happened occasionally, until the principles of corporate management were misapplied to reorganised local authorities in 1973, with education budgets put in their place or fighting their corner with other service spending both in central and local government, whilst schools and other services in any one locality were excluded. It was not just school governing bodies which were excluded from financial deliberation; the Department of Education and Science was not the source of funding and has had no resource of expertise in this field, being a divided house with reduced communication between civil servants drawn in from the Treasury to curb spending but with no knowledge of education, and Her Majesty's Inspectorate drawn from curricular areas of the education service, often before gaining significant involvement in the management of schools or services as a whole. Education departments in local authorities have been similarly limited, and have had to learn on the job how to put their case through the Treasurer or Chief Executive to a local authority policy and resource committee. Devolution of financial responsibility to schools from central or local education departments is a move from one location of generalists to another, not from professionals to amateurs. Centrally-held statistics are inadequate and evidence offered by HMI too unstructured to form a firm basis for funding any one part of the service. Local authorities rarely hold coherent records which would enable them to plan for the future.

Right through to the 1980s, there were some local authorities which contrived not to have governing bodies distinct from the education committee itself or its schools sub-committee. In the politics of the Headmasters' Association from the late 1960s and then from 1978 for the Secondary Heads Association, much time was spent up and down the country arguing with a sizeable minority of local authorities across the political spectrum, in the attempt to have genuine governing bodies for each school, a feature of secondary (grammar) schools pre-war which the 1944 Act was obviously intended to extend. Heads on the whole have wanted to be responsible to their own school governing body, and have also wanted a governing body to share in representing the needs of the school to the local authority. Policy statements from the heads' associations were consistent in this.

2 Growth and spending in the 1960s

There is little doubt that the main promptings for schools to be alert to costs and to have a larger measure of control over them has come from school heads and principals. Many of the local authority schemes now developing are the result of years of school pressure. The pressure was prompted by rapid growth and development in the 1960s. Education was set fair to overtake armaments as the largest item of the national budget; the school-leaving age was about to be raised; curriculum development was being promoted with funding from government and other sources; on the whole, enterprising schools received what they asked for and therefore acquired the habit and skills of asking. Reorganisation to comprehensive schooling, accompanied by the baby boom, gave opportunity for further spending on developments, but at the same time required skills to persuade councils that there would be economies of scale and site. In many of the smaller local authorities – this was before local government reorganisation increased their size and reduced their number – experience of comprehensive schooling was not to be found in the office but in those appointed to run the schools, and there was considerable reliance on heads to state and to share in costing what would be the needs of the new institutions, an opportunity which was not lost. Heads and deputies were involved in everything from building design to furniture costs, as part and parcel of organisational and curricular development, making the first major reorganisation proposals on the basis of complete knowledge of costings for the whole service, possible sources of funds, transfer across budgets as diverse as school transport and science laboratories.

3 Improvement without growth

Perhaps during the 1960s and early 1970s it was those who were heads in areas of static population, where developments of good practice had to be promoted without the excuse of additional numbers and government sanction for major building development, who became most acutely aware of the scope for 'viring' funds, for making savings on previous practice in order to promote improvement. There was, for example, the group of us beavering away in the backwaters of Somerset, which was untouched by the baby boom. Brian Knight was by 1970 sharing thoughts from Chard on the unit costs of teaching, on the maintenance overheads of school travel and buildings, and on ways of shifting savings from one to the other. I was at the same time making estimates from Minehead of the real costs of school examinations, on the costs and functions of non-teaching staff in schools; and we were combining to emphasise as a major responsibility of headship the control of the physical environment of learning. Another group of us as heads in the south-west were setting down guidelines for school buildings (HMA, 1968), not previously a central concern of professional policy emanating from schools, but now derived from a wealth of experience derived from the drawing boards for comprehensive schools in each area. As heads, we were quite literally on the drawing board.

4   Competition across sectors

Financial wisdom was also becoming a necessary political tool for those who were running institutions. The 104 local authorities were being sucked into the norms of costing as developed by CIPFA; if school heads did not have access or understanding of the CIPFA figures, they were without the language for financial presentation. There was, moreover, an unfortunate and unnecessary difference in the habits of schools and further education colleges; the latter collected money direct from part-time students and for some vocational courses from clients in industry. Ironically, they had more sight of their money but were more constrained than schools in how to use it, each individual course having to be viable. In the late 1960s, as part of the raising of the school-leaving age, there emerged the further education alternatives to 'all-through' secondary schools. Was the 'tertiary' solution a better structure within which to promote comprehensive life-long learning? Every secondary school and every technical college became involved in acrimonious argument, usually described as 'partnership', to justify maintaining or increasing their share of the population. Unit costs were a key part of that argument.

Heads for the first time had to have their hands on the information of unit costs, and be able to use it, particularly in the area of 16–19 education. Again, the Department of Education and Science was without the expertise to offer guidance, and employed an accountancy firm to try to help; but the evidence of Arthur Young & Co. was as inconclusive as had been that of another leading accountancy firm, Peat Marwick, a few years before.

5   Keeping priorities from cuts

To these pressures to acquire and apply the language of accountability were added from the mid-1970s that threefold decline which has dogged the schools service ever since: simultaneously, a decline in confidence in schools as a priority instrument of social and economic improvement; demographic decline as a result of more effective and accepted contraception; and economic decline affecting Great Britain in relation to its competitors. So schools were to have a smaller slice of a smaller cake for a smaller part of the population. The rate support grant from central to local government was consistently reduced but most erratically distributed from one year to the next as between urban and rural areas. Continuity of practice in any one local authority could no longer be guaranteed, both because of the changing political tactics of the Department of the Environment in administering the grant and because all local government had only since 1973 also become susceptible to party political swings and roundabouts.

Now if schools know anything, they know about a commitment to continuity for their pupils. Central and local government may be run on annual budgets, despite the recommendations of the Audit Commission; but schools have a commitment to complete programmes for pupils over five, six or seven years. So one of the first kinds of virement looked for is diachronic: carrying monies or a proportion of them across from one financial year to the next. This particular form of financial responsibility is the least understood from central government. Over the last twenty years, it has come to be better understood and applied locally. In many areas, schools no longer have to spend up in wild haste by the end of the financial year for fear of losing their balance, and in some it is accepted that they may have to overspend by an agreed percentage in order to secure resources or fund developments in advance of teaching programmes, and in order to effect long-term savings. But as soon as central government comes in with its 'initiatives', the wild spending has to start again. Developments funded by the Manpower Services Commission (or Training Agency) have been perceived to be wasteful in this respect; government funding for in-service education is similarly restrictive.

Cuts from the mid-1970s left schools and education offices with a dilemma: it was the officers who had to trade through the local authority machine to secure budgets for the schools; and they needed to have control of spending in order to justify it. On the other hand, when cuts were forced upon the service despite their efforts, it made sense to pass them on to the schools to make the best they could of a bad job. In schools, there were many who wished to be seen to keep their hands clean. School responsibility for finance, they considered, would be fine at times when there was enough money to do the essential job; when there was not, the employer should bear the brunt of criticism. Others, however, argued that it was in the interests of children to have the least possible damage done; those on the spot were responsible for ensuring that; it was precisely when there was difficulty that real responsibility could and should be exercised; and local financial management should be seen to work in the most adverse circumstances in order to give confidence in school responsibility whatever the circumstances.

6   Retrieving good practice from local government reorganisation

Local government reorganisation brought smaller local authorities which had each developed some forms of devolution practice: 'flexibility allowances' with a proportion of school finances offering choice across equipment, part-time and non-teaching staff. In other, governing bodies of secondary schools had had the responsibility of drawing up full estimates, informed as needed by the city education department. That practice was the first to disappear; there was no place for governing bodies in whole-service corporate management. Then 'flexibility' became the first victim of cuts; the areas of option became 'extras', then non-essentials, and then disappeared. In the mid-1970s, heads and governors were looking for a restoration of flexibility and virement, precisely because of the cuts and despite the reluctance to take responsibility for them. In its local financial clauses, the legislation of 1986 and 1988 is doing no more than restoring and spreading some sensible elements of previous good practice, to make sense of spending on site.

7   The size of schools

There have been further important factors in the professional moves towards site responsibility for financial management. The first is school size. The early arguments for comprehensive education were accompanied by a belief in economies of scale. Secondary schools grew larger rather than more numerous to meet the expanding population and age-span. The larger and the more complex an organisation, the greater are the opportunities for permutation within it. These can only be exploited if the organisation is freed from simplistic formulae imposed from outside. Moreover, they cannot be understood or perceived from outside; responsibility for determining priorities and viring funds has to be taken and indeed further distributed internally by the institution itself. Some individual items do, however, become self-evident. In a large school, repairs are not individual items but accumulate into a constant demand for a general handyperson presence; energy savings are not only 'educational', but represent considerable sums which could be better spent on other school activities. If a school can make the transfer, and has the responsibility to do so, it will have the incentive to propose the obvious and to try to make it work. So too with staff cover: if the level of staff absence averages 2 per cent for all reasons and there are two hundred adults, it is more likely that a school will want to add a small number to the permanent staff rather than chase through an education department supply list for occasional cover every time an absence occurs. There is nothing remarkable in all this: seen from the school, it is plain common sense, whereas in a local authority department where each section concentrates on one budget heading and is dealing at the same time with small and large organisations, all called schools, a single system will work to the lowest common denominator.

8   Resourcing to reduce disadvantage

Another major influence has been awareness of special need and deprivation. Central government attempts to 'level' up by positive discrimination have been clumsy. They have included the designation of education priority areas (EPAs) and extra staff and funding for EPA schools; the problem with these was a failure to recognise or be able to identify the continuum of need. Another device was to designate 'schools of exceptional difficulty', with extra payment for running them. Presumably it was in the financial interest of heads to have the school remain difficult to run. A third element was extra weighting in rate support grants from central to local government: one weighting for central London, another for LEAs in the vicinity, and no weighting for those outside. Again, anomalies arose wherever the lines were drawn and whenever they were changed.

Meanwhile, serious attempts were being made to find means of distributing public funding according to need. There was useful research in the early 1970s, resulting in social indexing. It became clear that there was a close correlation between social deprivation and educational need. In the mid-1970s, the Association of Head-mistresses and the Headmasters' Association, before their amalgamation, combined to project a document entitled 'When will they ever learn?', which adopted social indexing and recommended how to use it for resourcing schools. This was a significant departure from the spurious equality of the same per capita staffing and resourcing in any one LEA, whatever the circumstances of the school or its population. It was also the element missing in the Warnock Committee's report (DES, 1978) on special educational needs. Social indexing was adopted by some LEAs as the basis of various measures of financial flexibility to schools. The ILEA Additional Use of Resources scheme is the most significant of these, and the social indexing on which it is based remains one of the most carefully thought through. Here again, it is unfortunate that special educational needs have been separately categorised and funded. The resource approach to meeting all needs, with a background of practice in the USA, allied to a whole-school approach to meeting needs, depends on local management of resources.

9   School and community

A third major element has been the development of community schools. As indicated earlier, what is meant by community schools varies widely across the country. At a basic level, we may be talking of community access to the use of school facilities. If there are booking arrangements and fees to be paid to a remote education department, involving the school in making all the arrangements without return or responsibility, there are bound to be barriers, not least in the caretaking. Where, anyway, does school extra-curricular activity end and community booking begin? Where does separately organised youth and adult education fit in? It is simply good sense for the whole transaction, including the financial side, to be conducted in the school itself.

That may fit well with the view that schools should in any case be so organised as to include all such activities anyway. The Cambridgeshire Village College movement, which touched many parts of the country and is perhaps most clearly updated in the Leicestershire Community College schemes, provides much clearer evidence of local financial management, involving the whole community, than do the more recently publicised 'pilot' schemes. It is no small wonder that those associated with the management of community education as a whole see the present proposals from government as an excellent opportunity, whatever the intentions behind it. On the other hand, the explicit exclusion of adult education and the option of passing school property to leisure and recreation services could distort responses.

10   Schools and parents

With or without policies of community schooling, most schools have had the support of parents in promoting and paying for activities inadequately resourced from the public purse. Some have been channelled through parent-teacher association fund-raising activities; some have been through a general levy or school subscription; others have been through individual payment for school visits, musical instruments and tuition, plays, concerts, sport activities, clubs, residential education opportunities, camps, ski trips, language exchanges, materials for home economics and other practical subjects. Until recently, these contributions were made within the confines of what might be called the icing on the cake; the local authority would and should provide the essentials; parents would wish to enhance essentials without detracting from the local authority's responsibility. It is what industry would call 'hearts and flowers' donations. The recent attempt to provide government regulations for the funding of such activities may clarify the issue but does nothing to solve the problem.

What had always been evident to anyone who chose to look more closely became apparent to everyone through the recent decade of cutbacks in public funding: there was never that clear distinction to be made between essential services and desirable extras, between overt and hidden curriculum, between work and encouragement.

Schools were just not being painted; should the parents lend a hand to stop the rot? Books were not being supplied in adequate numbers to be brought home. Should parents make good the deficiency? If they did, would local authorities expect them to, and provide even less? Parents needed to know what local authorities were up to, in order to decide what they could best do about it. In many schools, by no means just in a privileged area, corporate fund-raising and contributions in kind from parents was consistently doubling the money provided from public funds for books, stationery and equipment. Should the school plan with that in mind or pretend it was not happening?

There was always the argument that to promote contributions from parents and other local interest groups would increase inequalities between schools. It was difficult to sustain when one looked at the differences in funding anyway from one local authority to another; and instead of seeing such contributions as the thin end of the wedge, it is perfectly possible to accept and encourage what people want to give, on the understanding that the school or local authority might balance this out if it left others at a disadvantage.

All these are everyday examples of what headship was about in the 1970s. What was needed and is now emerging was a negotiated scheme which would bring together such individual elements and experiences into an acknowledged scheme across schools. The case was made by the Audit Commission, set up in 1983 to improve local authority financial management. One of its first acts was to study non-teaching costs in secondary schools and to publish a report in 1984 setting out very firmly the case for financial devolution to schools, and pointing out that heads often in fact already exercised most of the areas of decision which caused money to be spent. Meanwhile, some local authorities were developing pilot schemes. They included: the Inner London Education Authority, whose Additional Use of Resources scheme started in 1973 and was based on school circumstances and a social index of positive action; Solihull, where a pilot scheme for six schools was started in 1981; Cambridgeshire, where six secondary schools and one primary school were involved in a pilot scheme starting in 1982 and then extended to all secondary schools and a larger group of primary schools; Cheshire, where a pilot scheme in 1983 was followed by inclusion of all secondary schools by 1984 in a very modest and gradual scheme; East Sussex, where from the 1983 pilot scheme, most secondary schools, one further education college and several primary schools are now taking part in a scheme similar to Cheshire's; Surrey, with five schools and one college starting in a pilot scheme in 1985; Oxfordshire, with a shadow exercise in 1984 preceded by individual energy and building incentive projects and followed in 1985 by a pilot scheme across five volunteering schools; and Lincolnshire, whose pilot scheme started across seven schools. These have since been extended and joined by several further local authority schemes.

Dispelling current myths

Earlier, it was suggested that there were four widely held views about local financial management: that it was novel, that it was right wing, that it would give more power to heads, and that it would take more time in schools. The evidence and experience suggest that none of these need be true. This chapter has already sketched past practice on which to build. What of the other three views?

1   LFM and political stances

The local authorities which introduced schemes for school 'virement', or flexibility across specific budget headings, including staff costs, were and still are across the political spectrum. The most significant of them has been the largely Labour-controlled Inner London Education Authority's 'Additional Use of Resources' (AUR) scheme. Other schemes for 'flexibility allowances' were driven out by the education cuts which began to be felt from 1977, first in Conservative shires deprived of central grant by a Labour government priority for inner city areas; and then by Labour authorities squeezed by a Conservative government from 1979. Current Conservative legislation includes politically contentious and divisive proposals: but the opposition parties are not questioning the principle of financial devolution. In Cambridgeshire, one of the local authorities seen to be piloting the most recent schemes, politicians have quarrelled not so much about the scheme, but about which of them invented it. In Oxfordshire, the first proposal for significant virement to a school was from a Labour-controlled governing body to a Conservative authority in 1976; it was piloted in a reversed political context by governing bodies which had changed complexion in a local authority in which control had also changed in the opposite direction. Support and reservations are to be found on all sides.

Just as the main force for returning or devolving financial responsibility to schools has been a politically neutral management principle, so was the main force for removing it earlier. The main force against school financial responsibility was the flawed introduction into the local authorities of corporate management across services, following the Bains Report (1972). Neither in central government grants nor within local government is there a separate education budget; a block grant to support local taxation is made for the corporate local authority service from the Department of the Environment. If a local education service does not have its own budgetary continuity, its officers are sucked into a corporate inter-service structure whilst the schools remain isolated in a specific and financially subordinate one. Corporate management is not in itself a faulty management principle; but it was applied at all points except the one that mattered, where schools, social and other services should be combining to serve their locality.

The present Government is at the same time looking towards privatisation of some existing public services and more centralist in managing such public services as it wishes to retain; it is less favourably inclined towards local authorities than have been any of its predecessors, and its promotion of local financial management by schools is in a context of pressures to reduce local government powers and services; but there are those on the left wing of British educational politics who have been even blunter in their proposals. In 1983, A. H. Halsey, that doyen of the left and committed proponent of a complete system of comprehensive schooling, was putting it this way:

> Without abrupt departure from the custom of mixed central and local taxation, we could, in British terminology, begin by making every school a direct grant school. School government could be simultaneously reformed along the lines recommended in the Taylor Report. A central national administration, but a slimmer one, would remain with three main tasks: to administer the direct grant formula, to collect and disseminate information on the performance of the education system, and to inspect. The LEAs, with their apparatus of administration, advice and control over finance and appointments, would go. Schools governing bodies would govern, and be answerable to their electorate in the local community and the school itself.

It is too early to state how far local authorities will be deprived of the political responsibility to decide what amounts of money should be allocated to each school in the first place. That, rather than how it is spent, is the test of political control and social direction. So we shall expect some authorities to allocate budgets which include scales of weighting according to identified need, that is to say which reflect positive discrimination in favour of the socially deprived, whilst others will adopt a different view of 'fairness' and allocate more strictly on a per capita basis. The intention, initially, is that at least 75 per cent of the schools budget should be allocated on an age-weighted per capita basis. However, age-weighting proposals are also affected by social policy.

2   More power to the head?

Some voices have been raised in the teacher unions and elsewhere, more by habit than out of conviction, in protest against giving more power to heads over their staff. But pilot schemes for school financial management have in fact spread the responsibility across the school staff; where previously heads may have kept the money under wraps, there now has to be open consultation about proposals to vire between budget headings, especially if staffing is involved, and that brings teaching and non-teaching unions into the school's decision making considerably more than before. Moreover, it is a caricature of such schemes to suggest that they give power to the head and staff; governing bodies, now to represent the whole local community, including the teachers in a school, have always been as powerfully involved as they chose to be, and are now to be required to receive spending proposals and to take responsibility.

3 More school time spent on financial control?

In recent years, local authority budgets have been carved into specific funding for particular sections of the education and other depart-ments. In any one county or town hall, a different person in a different office will hold the purse strings for as many as thirty different activities all of which form a part of a school's organisation. The head of a school has either been spending inordinate amounts of time trying to locate such people, trying to get each of them to understand the school context and connections with other budgets, trying to persuade them each to give priority to a particular school problem or proposal, or will have been considered unsupportive in straitened circumstances, by staff, parents and governors. Many of us who spent the 1970s pleading for a return to school responsibility were motivated by sheer frustration at the amount of time wasted in getting through the system, and by anger at the amount of money being wasted and the imbalance of priorities in spending on specific budgets without reference to a context which could only be perceived by those working in the school.

Some of the recent pilot schemes – in Solihull and in Cambridge-shire – have been more time-consuming for schools than they should have been; but in others, including the one with which I was pre-viously associated in Oxfordshire, quite simply micro-technology support has considerably reduced the school time spent on money matters before the scheme was introduced. Local authorities have since been combining with micro-technology firms to produce soft-ware appropriate to the national scheme. It is a myth to suggest that in a devolved financial system heads will need financial management skills which they have not already had to acquire. Eventually, they may not have to be as proficient in treasure-hunting in the catacombs of county or town halls.

Unfortunately, because local financial management has coincided with the acquisition by central government of powers to make specific grants outside the scheme, and because different local authorities will wish to retain discretionary powers over different budgetary items, the treasure-hunting for public funds will not be greatly reduced in the early years, whilst the search for voluntary funds is likely to increase. Local financial delegation is being presented as a rational management scheme; but rationality is confused with the entrepreneurial promptings of contemporary politics. The following list of sources of funds (see Figures 7a and 7b) for which schools will still have to go hunting is not exhaustive; but it could be exhausting if some further rational criteria were not quickly applied. Items A-C are included in the Government statement of its scheme, but will depend on LEA distribution; items D and E, shown in capitals, have to be added to the list. The most important of all are those mentioned last.

Conclusion

There is considerable resistance to schemes imposed by central government. Staff appraisal, for example, has been wanted by the unions, but it has been the imposition by a government which does not acknowledge professional goodwill which has been resisted. Salary scales and conditions of service are not gladly accepted because they were imposed; but they are almost identical to those which were negotiated between local employing authorities and unions before the government withdrew teachers' and employers' negotiating rights.

I do not think the same fate awaits local financial management. Part of the 1988 legislation, affecting all secondary schools and the larger primary schools, but not requiring the inclusion of special schools, does require local authorities to have a scheme; and it is tighter than the wording of the initial consultative document, which was reasonably flexible and not seriously opposed. However, tighter regulations are there to be modified. There has to be responsiveness on all sides as schemes are tried out. The local pilot schemes have been initiated usually in voluntary pilot schools; the question remains whether local financial management will prosper when extended across all schools and colleges, whether initiated from central or local authorities. They will prosper if schools can feel ownership without assuming proprietary power.

Essential in any scheme is the full support of the head, staff and governing body of each school. That support will depend on two major conditions. The first is that there should be seen to be direct potential benefit to the school and its pupils. So there have to be built-in incentives. The second is that it should be a management tool capable of developing the aims of the schools, and in keeping with their value systems. That will depend in part on the basis for the school budget in the first place and partly on the process of

A. GOVT SPECIFIC GRANTS

e.g.

- Education Support Grant
- LEA Training Grants
- Urban Aid Projects
- TVEI Extension
- Careers Service Funds
- Micro-Technology Funding
- Home Office Section 11 Staffing

B. LEA MONEY OUTSIDE THE GENERAL SCHOOLS BUDGET

e.g.

- Nursery
- Adult, Youth and Community
- Incentive Schemes

MANDATORY EXCEPTIONS

=

Capital Expenditure
Central LEA Administration
Inspectors, Advisers
Home — School Transport

C. DISCRETIONARY EXCEPTIONS

any of:

School Meals
Structural Repairs and Maintenance
Services — Ed. Psych, EWO, Pupil Support Staff,
to Pupils   Adv. and Peripatetic Teachers, Special
    Units, Resources for 'Statements'
LEA Initiatives
Added Staffing Costs —'Safeguarding'. Some 'Cover,'
    JP and Union Official Time
    Premature Retirements, Dismissals
Insurance for Premises, Equipment, Governors
Contingencies — Large overall changes in pupil numbers
    — Unpredicted increases in costs
    — Allowance for errors
    — Emergencies

D. FROM OTHER PUBLIC SERVICES

OTHER SCHOOLS AND COLLEGES, MUTUAL AID
LEISURE AND RECREATION,ARTS COUNCIL,
    SPORTS COUNCIL
SOCIAL SERVICES
HEALTH SERVICES
POLICE
(DEFENCE)
ENVIRONMENT
REFUSE COLLECTION

Figure 7a *Sources of funds or resources to be sought from non-delegated public service budgets*

E. VOLUNTARY SOURCES

LARGE INDUSTRY AND COMMERCE

   TRAINING
   EDUCATION RESOURCES
   WORK EXPERIENCE
   COMPACT
   SCHOOL BANK?
   GENERAL ADMIN. EQUIPMENT
   ADVERTISEMENT?

PUPILS

   CARE OF RESOURCES
   SELF-SUPPORT STUDY
   ENERGY SAVING
   SCHOOL MAINTENANCE
   WORK EXPERIENCE

SMALL BUSINESS

   SUPPLIES AND HELP AT COST
   ADVERTISEMENT?
   PUBLICITY
   WORK EXPERIENCE
   BUSINESS DEALS

PARENTS

   PUPIL EQUIPMENT
   VOLUNTARY FUNDS
   FUND-RAISING
   INVOLVEMENT

VOLUNTARY ORGANISATIONS

   MUTUAL HELP
   EDUCATION RESOURCES
   INSTRUCTION
   GRANTS
   ACTIVITIES

GOVERNORS

   INVOLVEMENT
   CHARITABLE FOUNDATION?

VOLUNTARY HELPERS

   ACTIVITIES
   ANCILLARY SUPPORT
   SOME MAINTENANCE
   REPAIRS

TEACHERS

   THAT HUGE SOURCE OF
   COMMITMENT BEYOND
   1265 HOURS

PREMISES, EQUIPMENT

   INCOME FROM LETTINGS
   SALES

NON-TEACHING COLLEAGUES

ditto

Figure 7b *Sources of funds or resources to be sought from voluntary bodies* decision making within and around the schools. Local financial management may, then, lend itself to a variety of political and social directions, and to a variety of management styles.

Local financial management is not a panacea. In education as in any other context, decisions are best taken as close as possible to the point of action, and action is most likely to be effective where people share all aspects of responsibility. The location of financial responsibility does not make much immediate difference to the total amounts available; but it does enable educators to spend where spending is most necessary, and to equip themselves with the language of resourcing to explain and justify the need for it.

In a deeper sense, it is a necessary part of an education process. You cannot credibly be educating young people towards cooperative decision making and autonomy without showing that you have it in the school's organisation. It is a high profile part of the supposedly hidden curriculum. It could become part of the overt curriculum; young people should not have to go elsewhere to discover the workings of the world of work. Schools are visible workplaces with value systems.

SEVEN

Developing the Heart of Schools

The heart is a difficult word. I am choosing it deliberately, in almost a theological connotation, to mean the very core of a school's being. It also has the meaning of good spirit, taking heart, and that too has to be writ large in the coming decade. It contrasts with the head, either in the meaning of the person at the top or in the meaning of rational systems. 'The heart has its reasons which reason knoweth not.' We need to find the reasons at the heart of a school in order to develop management appropriately or effectively. As well as keeping up, receiving, reacting, responding with cerebral fever, people in schools have to delve down and discover what in their heart of hearts they mean to be and mean to do. There are styles of management which may assist, and others which may prevent groups of people going to the grounds of being and translating values into action in changing contexts. That also has a bearing on strategies and practices in developing management.

The prevalent model: training at the top

Management training for schools has been conceived by government as management at the top, as the training of heads and senior staff. There are any one of three possible reasons for this. Partly, there is the 'boss' mentality. That does not exclude the 'good boss' consulting and developing 'staff' in general or the senior management team in particular. But it has also been thought necessary to strengthen 'management' faced with a more effectively unionised workforce; so there have been funded projects to develop training in staff management conceived in terms of control and industrial dispute.

Secondly, there is the lingering assumption that there is a distinct break between the role of the teacher in the classroom with pupils and the head or head and deputies running the organisation which enables teaching and learning to happen. There has been frequent criticism of appointment to headship only on the basis of successful teaching; but certainly in comprehensive schools, that has been no more than a legend in the last two decades. In other countries it has remained more true than in Britain; it is reasonable in France or Czechoslovakia, say, to nominate teachers as potential heads and to train them in a nationally recognised system before they are appointed, if only because the job of a teacher there is to teach in the formal programme and very little more – not even to be on the premises for any other reason or at any other time. Many of the recently imposed conditions of service for teachers appear to exclude the head, and there is some drift towards the head as 'employer'. If that were what we wanted, it would be logical to press further for systematic re-training as a qualification for headship, together with other chief executive jobs, such as chief education officer or possibly chief inspector.

Thirdly, in fairness to the initiative which many of us pressed on Sir Keith Joseph and which carried through the years 1983–86, the training of heads and senior staff has been conceived in 'cascade' terms, with the hope that heads and deputies would then be able to train up other levels of management in the schools. This Bell and Lancaster mode translated into the staffroom is after all what used to happen in the elementary schools of the late nineteenth century before there was any other training for assistant teachers, and we can see it operating across the routines of chain store retail outlets today. There has even been some seal of approval on the cascade model from Her Majesty's Inspectorate, commenting recently (and perhaps hastily) on the speed-training to introduce GCSE. However that may be, it is of course highly questionable whether the managing director of any organisation is in the best position to be the training officer as well.

The effects of this kind of 'top-down' management training on schools have not been properly evaluated. The 1983 training opportunities have been welcomed at a time when it has not been easy to hold schools together. Individuals going through the various processes available have been grateful and empowered, whether the training has been off-site and individual or on-site and involving a senior group; if it has enabled them to cope better, it can be assumed that there is some benefit to those around them, but beyond that general assumption the effects on their colleagues or on the school as a whole has not been gauged. Yet government funding for training in organisation and management is still couched in terms of heads and senior staff, and local authorities which support management training for other 'levels' are very much in the minority. This 'top-down' model is being perpetuated within the system and to it is added an 'out-in' model from other government departments and industry. Within the system, there has at last been a development across fourteen local authorities in the South-East and central government, establishing a scheme to identify management training needs and opportunities; but it is still limited in its brief to the management training of school heads and senior staff, which remain the confines of government priority funding. This narrow view is being reinforced by proposals borrowed from other organisational cultures including school systems abroad for a clear break by training and accreditation between the job of teaching and the job of headship. Beyond the education system, the Department of Trade and Industry has initiated a national teacher placement scheme in industry, with the hope that good management practice may be seen in action and transferred. This is in the teeth of research evidence which suggests that on the whole industry is managed worse than are schools. There is much to be said for interchange of people and ideas across different zones of employment: but the emphasis has to be on interchange and on critical review which will be of use not only to those observing but to those observed.

Making management central

There are various reasons to propose a change of focus towards the centre of the school. One has to do with the sandglass image again; another with career progression in the education service; and both of these have to relate to the kind of school and the kind of service which is wanted.

First the sandglass. There is that narrow filter between the teaching-learning life of a school and the running of the organisation, a frequently blocked channel which many would wish to see freed and broadened. The trickle between the two parts of the sandglass depends very much on those whose job is in both parts: the teamleaders responsible for an area of the curricular programme and at the same time expected by their fellow teachers to secure in the organisation an adequate framework and resource for them to do their work. The same applies to those who have responsibility for a part of the school, perhaps a year or house or similar division. These are the communicators, the negotiators. In order to communicate, they have to have first-hand acquaintance with the teaching and learning and also with the whole context of school priorities through which to negotiate. Because that is their unique position, they are the most likely source of worthwhile and practical initiatives for change, given half a chance. And if they are not the source, they are the necessary bearers of change and development, which just will not happen unless they pick it up and carry it forward. Those in an area which might in hierarchical terms be described as middle management are, by definition, closer to every other point of the whole organisation than anyone else could or should be.

It may be argued that the sandglass is an inadequate image, and illustrates only the internal organisation of schools, and that middle management, whilst being the filter between the classroom and the school organisation, are not in the 'hinge' position between the school and its local or national context, which is so important in the management function. That is a wrong argument. If it is a statement of what happens, then it is a statement of something which has to be changed. All teachers have to be directly aware of and involved in the wider context of their work in and through schools. The tutor is the filter between the home and school; the head of department is the filter between a group of teachers and subject teaching developments and good practice elsewhere; the youth and community tutor, the counsellor, the pastoral may well be the filter between school and other services; the staff governor (not the head) is the filter between staff and governing body; there is probably a professional tutor as filter between training services and identified school needs; the head of music is the filter between school and community music making, the head of physical education between school and community sports and physical pursuits. The list soon extends to everyone developing a professional role as teacher. Everyone is involved in boundary management, not just the head, and everyone in a school needs to develop the skills to work effectively within and from the school, managing outwards and working with those who are managing from what is perceived as the outside.

Secondly, there is the present shape of the education service. Currently, a move from teaching to local authority administration will typically be made by teachers in their late twenties, after the initial experience of a full teaching programme and perhaps with a first responsibility for the work of others. This coincides broadly with the decisions still having to be made mostly by women teachers either to break from full-time career teaching in order to bring up children or to struggle against a loaded system to combine or compromise career and family commitments, or to commit themselves entirely to the professional career. Teachers may move to the advisory service either from their late twenties through the somewhat perilous rapids of temporary advisory teacher work, or somewhat later from running a subject department to being a subject adviser, later to take on a more general responsibility. The national inspectorate recruits in the thirty-five to forty-five range. The national ministry otherwise recruits from a general civil service, and not usually from local authority administration. A move to further training for work as an educational psychologist will also be made after a very few years of teaching, as may be the hazardous moves, sometimes through short-term edu-

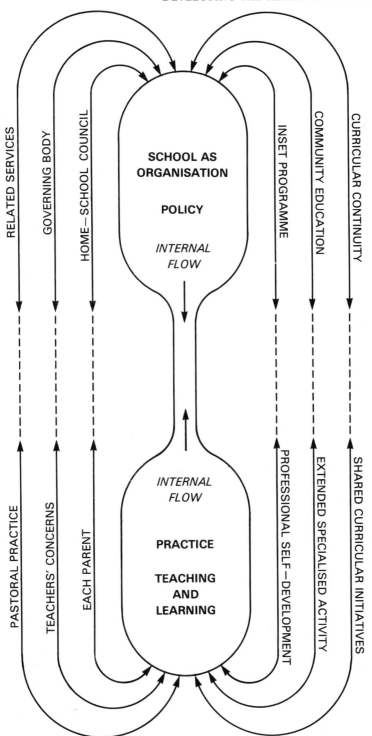

Figure 8 *Opening up the sandglass*

cational research to higher education including initial teacher-training.

There are of course examples of much later movement and cutting corners, but the general picture is one in which those who move out from schools to the other lines of the education service are unlikely to have had substantial training or experience in the organisation and management of the whole school in its wider context, especially if management is conceived of as a matter for heads and senior staff and if management training opportunities are centred on them.

Once the move is made, there are different organisational cultures, different unions (well over a dozen in the education service), and different patterns of management training. Junior administrative officers in education departments are shifted around sections rapidly to build up experience before taking responsibility for a section and moving towards the senior management team. They have some training opportunities at various levels, through local government as a whole, and through their professional association. Advisers and inspectors have had very little formal training, and the centre now set up for them at Woolley Hall is at least a gesture of recognition of their needs. Educational psychologists have been largely divorced from the management structures around them and from management development opportunities. Trainers of teachers, absurdly, have no recognisable training. The national inspectorate at least has a powerful mentor scheme followed by regular appraisal, and its team approaches are also an instrument for mutual development.

The general effect is of course to confirm and perpetuate the barriers across a divided service; one in which the divisions have no real understanding of each other; a service in which there is little scope for movement from schools after mid-career, and virtually no capacity for movement back into schools at any stage. Even more damagingly, the service then has planted upon it patterns of practice from management elsewhere which assume a very different background. So it is now assumed by senior civil servants that local authority advisers and inspectors will increasingly monitor and evaluate the performance of institutions and those who manage them; but they may well have had no experience of framing and working to complete whole school development plans, and have no credibility among heads or indeed among themselves as they are turned to this task, within a context of accountability by performance. Officers may become the chief executive of a local authority, and may be perceived to have some kind of authority over heads and some informed capacity to advise the council on matters affecting schools and colleges, without having had any previous experience of running an institution. Because they are the last to be extracted from schools and perhaps because they do not serve the same employer, national inspectors have had more credibility. Educational psychologists have credibility only in dealing with individual children, and are the last to be thought of as informing the management of the school learning process, curriculum development, or the social psychology of the school. Ministry civil servants are in a very different position now that central government has assumed not only ultimate powers but detailed executive and specific development roles; but their general background is as it was before, apart from a few brought in from industrial and accountancy management backgrounds, and only individuals emerge as recognisable contributors to the education service.

The alternative strategy

What we should be aiming for is first a whole professional service committed to a distinctive approach to educational management, in which there is no outmoded differentiation between teaching and managing, and in which it is acknowledged that schools and the education service are there to contribute to learning through living, and therefore have a shared responsibility with the other major centres of human activity: homes, communities, other places of work and leisure, other public services, other media. The management of cooperative and open professionality is part of the job of any teacher, not to be left only to those who move their priority away from teaching.

There are several ways to achieve that. First, if we want a professional service sharing respect and recognition across its various functions, we should go for a more flexible career structure, in which mobility is promoted not just away from teaching but to and from schools. I see no rhyme or reason in having separate salary structures for teachers, local advisers, national inspectors, psychologists, further and higher education teachers and teacher trainers, or officers. I see every reason for bringing them together into a united education service career.

Secondly, that key public service requires a single professional body, probably in the form of a general teaching council, which would reflect the shared public responsibility by including representatives of parents, governors, and other centres of employment, and which would be responsible for advising on qualifications, training, and the professional standards required of anyone practising at any point in the service.

Thirdly, professional development being conceived across the whole service, forms of training would be appropriately recast. Crucially, there should be a common basis of education management training at the career development take-off point, which is either the start of middle management in schools or may become the start of a development away from the school base. This might be from five years after the introduction to teaching, when there is a basis of personal experience and reflection from which to develop further skills in managing self, others, organisations, programmes and communications, in the same part of the service or a changed context. From this general management base there may be short specific training with a focus on particular tasks and functions in the different parts of the service; but the emphasis will always be on the communality of a shared service and on professional partnership across it and out from it.

This is not a cure-all prescription. It has to relate to a general will, of which a common basis of remuneration and conditions of service, a general teaching council, and a general practice of mobility and dissemination of good practice across the service become the habit rather than the exception. Other anomalies have to be corrected beforehand; for example, the practice of educational psychology has to be tied back into the general professional service whatever the career and development structures, simply because the insights into how children learn should be shared with all engaged in the enterprise of education, not left on the margins of special remediation.

Management and equal opportunities

So far I have suggested no alternative to the biggest weakness of all, the failure to plan for equal career development opportunities for women. In this case, equality is not a matter of the same for all but of positive action urgently needed. There is in many parts of the country a much greater awareness of the issues than existed a generation ago, but not much has been done about it. Again, the issue has been addressed largely from the 'top'. The top is, of course, important in terms of gestures and symbols. Along with others, I used to ask what was to be done about the imbalance of numbers of men and women in leadership positions: school heads, chief education officers, college principals, HMI, polytechnic directors, and vice-chancellors. The regional and local variations were sufficient to point to ways to right the balance in a profession which is unique in combining two elements: a majority of its members are women, and what it does about equal opportunities will affect the perceptions of all the next generation.

However, the rhetoric has not achieved much. The local authorities which have adopted a formal policy of equal opportunities in appointments are those which were previously achieving more anyway. Only one or two local authorities have offered young teachers a choice by moving to a policy of parental leave rather than just maternity leave, and parental leave would only be a significant choice if it covered all forms of employment. Whether the leave is for

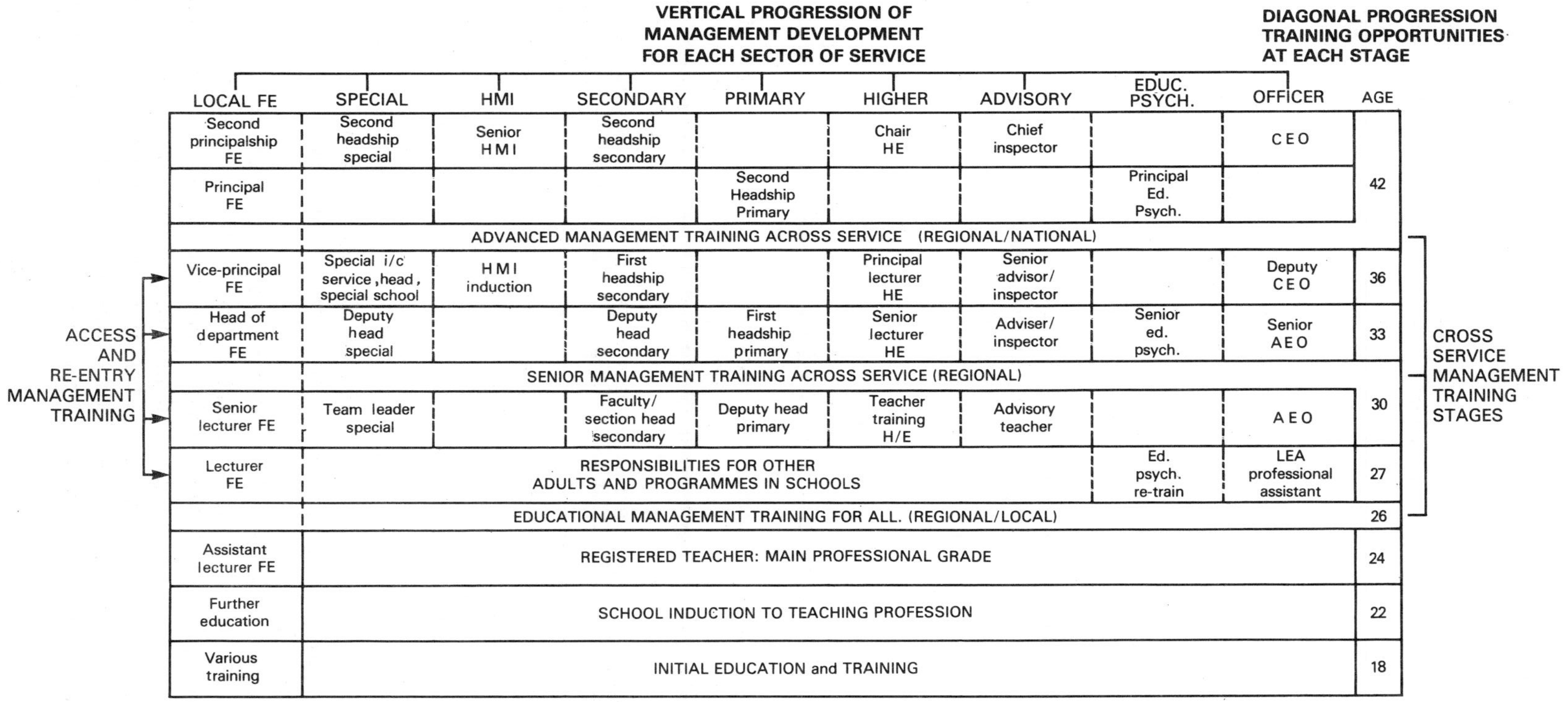

VERTICAL PROGRESSION OF
MANAGEMENT DEVELOPMENT
FOR EACH SECTOR OF SERVICE

DIAGONAL PROGRESSION
TRAINING OPPORTUNITIES
AT EACH STAGE

CROSS SERVICE MANAGEMENT TRAINING STAGES

LOCAL FE	SPECIAL	HMI	SECONDARY	PRIMARY	HIGHER	ADVISORY	EDUC. PSYCH.	OFFICER	AGE
Second principalship FE / Principal FE	Second headship special	Senior HMI	Second headship secondary	Second Headship Primary	Chair HE	Chief inspector	Principal Ed. Psych.	C E O	42
Vice-principal FE	Special i/c service, head, special school	HMI induction	First headship secondary		Principal lecturer HE	Senior advisor/inspector		Deputy C E O	36
Head of department FE	Deputy head special		Deputy head secondary	First headship primary	Senior lecturer HE	Adviser/inspector	Senior ed. psych.	Senior AEO	33
Senior lecturer FE	Team leader special		Faculty/section head secondary	Deputy head primary	Teacher training H/E	Advisory teacher		A E O	30
Lecturer FE							Ed. psych. re-train	LEA professional assistant	27
									26
Assistant lecturer FE									24
Further education									22
Various training									18

ADVANCED MANAGEMENT TRAINING ACROSS SERVICE (REGIONAL/NATIONAL)

SENIOR MANAGEMENT TRAINING ACROSS SERVICE (REGIONAL)

RESPONSIBILITIES FOR OTHER ADULTS AND PROGRAMMES IN SCHOOLS

EDUCATIONAL MANAGEMENT TRAINING FOR ALL. (REGIONAL/LOCAL)

REGISTERED TEACHER: MAIN PROFESSIONAL GRADE

SCHOOL INDUCTION TO TEACHING PROFESSION

INITIAL EDUCATION and TRAINING

ACCESS AND RE-ENTRY MANAGEMENT TRAINING

Figure 9 *Management development for a whole education service*

mothers or for either the mother or the father, our national scheme is among the most disgracefully inadequate in the developed world. In more civilised countries, not just those with more money in the system, leave with salary for one year is available across all jobs, with a further period of two years within which the mother (or parent) has the right to return to her post.

We should be pressing for that anyway, in any employment. The principal reasons for doing so are supported by economic reasons. Unless we at least level up the rights of women teachers by 1992 we are going to be the losers in the professional mobility which will develop across the European Communities. But in the education service, because of its unique position, we should be doing much more besides. It is the service which throws away more professional skills than any other by wasting the trained resource of women with children, even when we know that there are serious shortages already and that the dwindling supply of graduates will cause crisis in the future.

First, we must recognise that parental leave is a key part of any career and not just an interruption; that it adds to the learning experience and understanding of those employed to educate the young. At present, a 'return' to teaching, with all the pressures surrounding it, has either to be made within weeks to the post previously occupied, or the right to return is forfeited. A later 'return' is therefore usually to a post without the additional responsibility which may have attached to the previous post, and may well be to a temporary and/or part-time position. Crèche facilities attached to schools are the exception, and should be the rule. The professional treatment not just of part-time teachers but of supply teachers is appalling, not by intent but by sheer thoughtless neglect throughout the education system, even though there is a desperate shortage of supply teachers. Meanwhile, for a woman returning to teach, the whole career has to be rebuilt. There are no increments for childbearing as there would be for, say, employment in industry. That is a totally unacceptable state of affairs. Loss of career status by virtue of being a woman with children is intolerable. The home-based period should be looked on as a form of secondment.

Secondly, it follows that we must look to a 'return' not just to the career level previously reached, but to the level which would have been reached if instead of rearing a family the teacher had continued in school-based full-time employment. So it should be possible for a head of department reviewing her career to contemplate either a period of three more years continuing as head of department and at the same time preparing for deputy headship or the same period bearing children and at the same time preparing for deputy headship. That requires attitude change all round, and there is no suggestion that the bearing of children should not be the overriding priority;

but no more is there any suggestion that running the department should be anything but the overriding priority whilst preparing for career advancement.

Thirdly, as part of that change of attitude and assumption, we must recognise the continuing training needs of those teachers who for a period are home-based and not school-based, and we must apply the funding and the organisation of INSET accordingly. So whereas INSET is now directed at those in employment, and indeed usually in permanent full-time employment only, it should address the specific needs of those seconded for the home-based employment of bringing up infant children, and those attempting to move back gradually by part-time or supply teaching.

That will not be achieved overnight. But it is part of a strategy for management development which is aiming at those making decisions in mid-career rather than after the decisions have been made. A generic form of management training for teachers from the point at which they are to take responsibility for the work of others, as well as themselves, will also be available to women developing a career in the education service, either immediately before they have children (for the average time spent teaching before the first child is now significantly longer than it used to be) or as part of their training for re-entry. It is at this mid-career stage, moreover, that management training can most usefully be related to further qualification through part-time advanced study.

It may well be considered that other aspects of equal opportunities for promotion through the education service can also be developed through positive action at this earlier career stage, in order to combat the potential disadvantages of ethnic background, of physical handicap, of language background. If positive action is applied too late, it can easily arouse acute feelings of injustice all round.

What kind of management training?

Like all planned INSET, systematic management training is best conceived as not merely added on but added on to continuous learning experience drawn from actual practice. So there are two sides: first, to see and organise actual work as potential learning, and secondly to draw out the learning and develop from it. Much management training should be action-based, learner-directed, and context-embedded (the context being both present and future). In proposing a conscious shift of emphasis from the 'tops' of each career pyramid within the education service towards a common grounding of management training, from which to be able to adapt with the help of sharper specific training to different climbing routes in a single pyramid, I am of course proposing shifts of context. I am also proposing that after the common grounding there should be a careful balance of training focused on particular routes and of training across the network. So management development, like career development and like policy development, should be thought through together across the education service as a whole. But essentially, training and development will still be about identifying and developing personal management needs, about leadership styles and the management of others, about the management of plant and resources, the management of programmes, the development of whole organisations, systems management, and working across systems (see Figure 10).

The main effect of changing the focus of management training will be to empower the service as a whole and not just the tips of the icebergs, and to unite the management of learning and the management of enabling systems. Both aims are worth working towards. To this end, it may be worth proposing a re-conceptualised staff college as an adjunct to a general teaching council. This would not be just for school heads and senior staff, but for the education service as a whole. It would probably have regional locations, each being the powerhouse for regional identification of needs, opportunities and future development. It would relate to any existing staff college for a particular branch of the service, such as further education or advisers, and would have the task of identifying needs for other specific centres. What is important is that the education service should

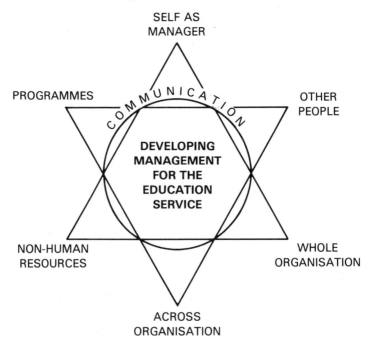

Figure 10 *A common grounding in management training*

be managed as a whole and should, as a whole, address the needs of each of its parts and the connections across them and from them to the whole educative community.

These are proposals which go to the heart of the education service. They are indeed pointing to a prescription for a new heart, through which to reach and be reached by every capillary of the system. But the heart has to be compatible with the whole body and with the activity which will be demanded of education as a corporate enterprise in the future. Major surgery may be required; but its purpose must be for the whole poisoned body to take heart. If we propound values of the kind suggested earlier in this book, we cannot live with management structures borrowed either from a more authoritarian past or from more authoritarian structures elsewhere in society. It is for the education service to identify and develop patterns of management which are effective for a democracy, and to convey these patterns across to other parts of the world of work.

A professional council for the education service

The education service has had many parts and therefore many divisions. There is, however, a deep professional and public commitment to an underlying unity of purpose, and there is an urgent need to establish a single recognised body with the authority to regulate and articulate those high professional standards and aspirations which will promote a teaching service of quality for future generations.

The General Teaching Council has existed in Scotland since 1966, and it is anomalous that England and Wales should still be left without this important element in the education service. The Committee, appointed by the Secretary of State for Education and chaired by Sir Toby Weaver, recommended in 1970 that a General Teaching Council should be established, and there has since that time been broad support in principle from ministers and opposition spokesmen, provided that there is agreement across the teaching profession and provided that the public interest will be served.

Broad agreement in principle has now been reached across seventeen major professional associations, and several other associations including those representing the public interest are now committed to joining the attempt to persuade the Government that the educating profession should take responsibility for recommending the development of its public service and for maintaining the professional standards expected in a key area. The self-managing outward-looking school makes best sense within a self-managing outward-looking profession.

What follows as an appendix is broadly the original text of the statement presented to the Secretary of State on behalf of this large forum of associations as a basis for action. Initially, the Council would focus on the training, registration and development of school teachers. But its proposed composition, to be negotiated in detail with all the identified interest groups including government, reflects the broader view of the educating profession and representatives of parents, governors, employers of teachers, and other sectors of employment. That should be our aim at all levels of education service for the future.

Appendix: The Proposed General Teaching Council*

Roles and functions for the General Teaching Council

The roles and functions for the General Teaching Council (GTC) will extend across:

- teachers' qualifications;
- the registration of those licensed to teach;
- the supply of teachers;
- the initial training of teachers;
- the induction of teachers;
- the in-service education and training of teachers;
- professional discipline;
- research related to the above; and
- external relations.

Salaries, pensions and conditions of service should remain firmly matters for negotiation between employers and unions.

The GTC will be the statutory independent professional governing body for the education service, analogous to the General Medical Council established by Parliament in 1858 and the GTC enacted for Scotland in 1965. It will represent a strong measure of self-government in professional matters and will, by stages, assume or subsume responsibilities previously held by various advisory bodies, together with the statutory powers to grant or withdraw registration to practise as a qualified teacher, in both the maintained and independent sectors. It will have, therefore, an overriding responsibility for maintaining standards within the profession, and for articulating information and advice about professional requirements, to its members, to the profession abroad, to the government, and to the public.

---

* This text, published in October 1988, is constantly revised, and updated versions are obtainable from the Universities' Council for the Education of Teachers.

Functions of the General Teaching Council

These will relate to:

1 The supply of teachers

The GTC will advise the Secretary of State on the numbers needed for entry to initial training in order to implement public policy for the service. Its advice will cover:

- national totals;
- age-phase;
- curricular areas; and
- the balance of modes of training (including re-training) most appropriate to the needs of the service.

2 The initial training of teachers

The GTC will determine:

- minimum qualifications for entry to initial training;
- the principles to be applied in devising selection procedures for initial training;
- the nature and length of initial training; and
- general criteria for the quality and coverage of initial training.

It will accredit existing and proposed courses of initial training according to the established criteria. It will decide on the acceptability of training and qualifications obtained outside England and Wales.

3 Registration

The GTC will be solely responsible for conferring a licence to teach, by registration with the Council. It will maintain the register of all persons so licensed to teach in England and Wales.

4 Professional discipline

The GTC will be committed to maintaining professional standards of conduct for registered teachers, in whatever capacity they may serve in the education service. The GTC will have the sole responsibility to withdraw Licensed Teacher status and to remove from the register, subject only to appeal to the High Court. It will have the sole right to reinstate as a registered teacher.

5 Entry to teaching

The GTC will assume responsibilities at present carried out by the Department of Education and Science under Teachers Regulations DES 1982 Schedule 6.

6 Initial service

The GTC will make recommendations on the general principles and long-term aims for professionally appropriate initial service, and will incorporate in its criteria for conferring licensed teacher status such regulations as may be established by law and such agreements on the initial service period as may from time to time be negotiated in relation to salaries and conditions of service between employers and unions. It will recommend appropriate professional standards of supervision of initial service. It will establish criteria for satisfactory completion of any such service. It will receive, approve and record recommendations on satisfactory completion of initial service, and will notify those concerned. The GTC will recommend good professional practice for the induction of teachers to their first post, within the framework of such entry conditions as shall have been negotiated by the appropriate bodies. The GTC will similarly recommend good practice for the induction of teachers to posts with significant change of responsibility, such as school headship, advisory, inspectoral or educational administration posts.

7 In-service education and training

The GTC will advise employers and the Secretary of State on the overall continuing training and development of teachers throughout their professional careers in the education service. The GTC will recommend on the accreditation of existing and proposed courses of in-service education and training designed to permit access to designated areas of the teaching profession.

8 Re-training

The GTC will advise employers and the Secretary of State on appropriate targets for numbers to be re-trained across curricular areas or age-phase. It will advise on appropriate provision of courses for such re-training, and on provision of re-training and other requirements for significant moves across senior levels of the education service.

9 Re-entry

The GTC will advise the Secretary of State and employers on targets for numbers to be drawn back to teaching from other careers or breaks in career; and it will advise on appropriate provision of courses and/or other requirements for successful re-entry or change of direction.

10 Research and enquiry

The GTC will promote research and enquiry in those professional fields which are closely related to the Council's role and functions.

11 External relations

The GTC will disseminate information and advice about the profession to its members, to the general public, to the media, and abroad. The GTC will make representations to the government and other major agencies, and will respond to consultative approaches in the professional fields within the Council's remit.

Registration

1 Principles and purposes of registration

The purpose of registration shall be to ensure an appropriately high level of relevant qualification, professional training and proven experience in the education service, such as to fulfil the public will for education of quality, and to control professional standards from within the profession, in order to be responsible for carrying out the service essential to the community. Registration according to agreed criteria, which may be varied as appropriate for teaching in particular parts of the education service, for example in further or higher education, shall be a condition for practice as a licensed teacher. Arrangements will be made for the assimilation of teachers qualified under previous dispensations. Rules for registration shall be subject to triennial review.

2 Stages leading to registration

(*a*) As a first stage, the Register shall include all those who teach in all recognised forms of primary and secondary education, and in professional elements of initial teacher-training. Inclusion on the Register shall be an entitlement for those qualified to teach in these parts of the service but who are not so doing. Qualification to be a provisionally registered teacher shall include:

(*i*) an appropriate level of attainment in general education, which shall also become the minimum requirement for entry to initial training;

(*ii*) completion of an accredited course of initial training at acceptable levels of attainment.

Registration to full membership shall follow satisfactory completion of a required period of initial service.

Note: Agreements made by the appropriate negotiating bodies before or after the establishment of the Council will be assimilated and re-interpreted in the criteria set up by the Council, which shall assume responsibility to review and re-define professional criteria for such classifications, except insofar as changes have a bearing on remuneration or conditions of service. Registration, and therefore eligibility to serve on the Council as well as the obligation to observe its codes of professional conduct, shall continue for those teachers who work, whether temporarily or permanently, in other parts of the education service for which experience as a qualified teacher is a normal pre-requisite for employment. These include, for example, employment as an education officer, adviser, inspector (including HMI), or educational psychologist.

(b) It shall be for the GTC once established to secure agreement on any separate categories, on any different requirements among them, or on different periods of transition or assimilation to the Register. Given the long-term aim to extend the coverage of registration across the whole professional education service, it will be particularly important to secure satisfactory arrangements for non-advanced further education, advanced further or higher education, youth and community service, and areas of development in vocational training across the 14–19 age-range.

(c) It shall be for the Council to determine any form of registration as a licensed associate, for example, among those employed as educational instructors in physical pursuits, instrumental music, the Youth Training Scheme, or in institutions which cannot be recognised or bound by professional criteria, such as commercial profit-making language schools.

Financing the General Teaching Council

1 There should be a detailed estimate of the costs of functions agreed for the GTC, in which assistance should be requested from the DES.

2 The government should contribute substantially to the initial costs of setting up the GTC.

3 The substantial initial registration fee should be included in the mandatory grant for initial teacher training, and passed direct to the GTC, subject to reimbursement for those who do not complete the course.

4 For existing teachers, there shall be a sliding scale for initial fee, related to years of remaining service.

5 There should be in addition a required annual subscription for

full membership, normally deducted at source and paid direct by the employer.

6 The Council shall have powers to fix the initial fee, subject to consultation with the Secretary of State, and to regulate annual subscription and such other charges as may be levied upon members.

7 The Council shall be entitled to receive public grants and other assistance, subject to the general principle of minimum dependence on government finance.

Relationship of GTC with government and other bodies

1 Government

(a) The GTC will be established by statute as an independent body serviced by its own secretariat, and therefore assuming powers and functions at present held by central government, such as recognition, approval of completed probation, and withdrawal of qualified status. This should involve some economies in central government, to be borne in mind in the recommended initial grant to the GTC.

(b) The Secretary of State will refer to the GTC for its views on matters for which in the past DES-supported advisory bodies have been used. It is envisaged that the GTC will have full access to the necessary government statistics and other information, and that this will not present problems, or cause significant additional work.

(c) HMI, itself a significant body of qualified teachers in a specific role, would develop a new relationship with the GTC across matters of professional discipline as well as accreditation, supply, INSET and possibly research.

(d) On matters of professional discipline, it will be the GTC and not the Secretary of State which will make decisions on matters referred to it from local negotiations; appeals relating to GTC decisions will be made to the High Court.

2 Professional associations

(a) Relationships with teachers' associations are reflected in the composition of the Council, which will decide on an appropriate balance of interests in its sub-groups. Arrangements will ensure that there will not be a conflict of interests between union or

124

employer representation on the GTC and support for particular members in matters of discipline, which will already have been dealt with in union-employer negotiation.

(b) Relationships with professional subject associations and other educational groups will be expected to develop in sub-groups and working parties related to their particular interests.

3 International and inter-professional work

(a) The GTC will establish liaison with comparable bodies in other countries, including the Scottish GTC, not least in determining international equivalence of qualification for teaching.

(b) It will exchange views with professional bodies for other public services, and will encourage inter-professional exchange of recommendations on work across services. It is to be expected that the GTC will be involved in harmonisation across the European Communities, in such matters as training and qualification.

4 Public relations

The GTC will have a major role in disseminating information about the teaching profession, and in responding to enquiries and comments about it.

Organisation of the Council

1 From the outset, the composition of the Council's governing body shall reflect the intended scope of its work in the long term, as laid down by Statute.

2 The GTC shall have in its governing body a clear majority of registered teachers. No one organised body should represent a majority.

3 The public interest, as represented by central and local government, by parents, governors and employment, shall be adequately represented, together with providers of training institutions.

4 It will be for the Council, once established, to determine its sub-groups and their appropriate composition, according to the functions they are to perform.

5 Decisions of the governing body shall be by a simple majority, except when a variation or extension of function is being proposed, within the framework laid down by Statute, when a two-thirds majority will be required.

Bibliography

ADVISORY COMMITTEE ON THE SUPPLY AND EDUCATION OF TEACHERS (1982) *The Initial Teacher Training System*. London: DES.

ADVISORY COMMITTEE ON THE SUPPLY AND EDUCATION OF TEACHERS (1984) *Teacher Training and Special Educational Needs*. London: DES.

ADVISORY COMMITTEE ON THE SUPPLY AND EDUCATION OF TEACHERS (1984) *The In-Service Education and Training of Teachers*. London: DES.

ARENDT, H (1986) *The Origins of Totalitarianism, London*: Deutsch (Andre) Ltd.

BELBIN, R. M. (1981) *Management Teams: Why they Succeed or Fail*. London: Heinemann.

BELL, A. (1797) *An Experiment in Education*. London: John Murray.

BAINS REPORT (1972). *The New Local Authorities: Management and Structure*. London: HMSO.

DE JOUVENEL, B. (1963) *Futuribles, Studies in Conjecture*. Geneva: Droz.

DEPARTMENT OF EDUCATION AND SCIENCE (1970) *A Teaching Council for England and Wales*. London: HMSO.

DEPARTMENT OF EDUCATION AND SCIENCE (1972) *The Education and Training of Teachers* (The James Committee). London: HMSO.

DEPARTMENT OF EDUCATION AND SCIENCE (1972) *A Framework for Expansion*. London: HMSO.

DEPARTMENT OF EDUCATION AND SCIENCE (1977) *Ten Good Schools: A Secondary School Enquiry*. London: HMSO.

DEPARTMENT OF EDUCATION AND SCIENCE (1978) *Special Needs in Education* (Warnock Report). London: HMSO.

DEPARTMENT OF EDUCATION AND SCIENCE (1978) *Making INSET Work*. London: HMSO.

DEPARTMENT OF EDUCATION AND SCIENCE (1981) *A View of the Curriculum*. London: HMSO.

DEPARTMENT OF EDUCATION AND SCIENCE (1982) *The New Teacher in School*. London: HMSO.

DEPARTMENT OF EDUCATION AND SCIENCE (1983) *Teaching Qualities*. London: HMSO.

DEPARTMENT OF EDUCATION AND SCIENCE (1988) *Secondary Schools*: An HMI Appraisal. London: HMSO.

DRUCKER, P. F. (1980) *Managing in Turbulent Times*. London: Heinemann.

FISHER, H. A. L. (1917) Statement introducing the Education Bill. London: Hansard.

HALSEY, A. H. (1983) 'Schools and Democracy' in AHIER, J. and FLUDE, M. (eds) *Contemporary Education Policy*. London: Croom Helm.

HANDY, C. B. (1984) *Taken for Granted: Looking at Schools as Organisations*. Harlow: Longman.

HARGREAVES, A. (1984) *Classrooms and Staffrooms: The Sociology of Teachers and Teaching*. Milton Keynes: Open University Press.

HEADMASTERS' ASSOCIATION (1968) *School Buildings*. London: HMA.

HILSUM, S. and STRONG, C. (1978) *The Secondary Teacher's Day*. Slough: NFER.

HOYLE, E. (1986) *The Politics of School Management*. London: Hodder and Stoughton.

HUGHES, M. (1973) 'The Professional as Administrator: the case of the secondary school head'. *Educational Administration Bulletin*, 2, 1.

INNER LONDON EDUCATION AUTHORITY (1985) *Educational Opportunities for All?* (The Fish Report). London: ILEA.

JOHN, D. W. (1980) *Leadership in Schools*. London: Heinemann.

JONES, A. (1987) *Leadership in Tomorrow's Schools*. Oxford: Basil Blackwell.

JONES, N. and SAYER, J. R. K. (1987) *Management and the Psychology of Schooling*. London: Falmer Press.

LABRIOLA, A. (1959) *Opere*. Milan: Feltrinelli.

LANCASTER, J. (1803) *Improvements in Education*. London.

MCCINTYRE, A. (1981) *After Virtue*. London: Duckworth.

OXFORDSHIRE EDUCATION DEPARTMENT (1988) *The Oxfordshire Skills Programme*. Oxford: Oxfordshire County Council.

ROYAL COMMISSION ON LOCAL GOVERNMENT IN ENGLAND (1969) Cmnd. 4039, (Redcliffe-Maud Report). London: HMSO.

RUSSELL, B. (1932) *Education and the Social Order*. London: George Allen and Unwin.

SAYER J. R. K. (1983) in BOOTH, T. and POTTS, P. (eds) *Integrating Special Education*. Oxford: Basil Blackwell.

SAYER, J. R. K. (1987) *Secondary Schools for All? Strategies for Special Needs*. London: Cassell.

SAYER, J. R. K. (1989) 'Teachers as Learners' in CLOUGH, E.; CLOUGH, P. and NIXON, J. *The New Learning: Programmes and Issues*. London: Macmillan.

SAYER, J. R. K. and JONES, N. (1985) *Teacher Training and Special Educational Needs*. London: Croom Helm.

TAYLOR REPORT (1977) *A New Partnership for our Schools*. London: HMSO.

UNIVERSITIES COUNCIL FOR THE EDUCATION OF TEACHERS (1988) 'A General Teaching Council for England and Wales: Consultative Document'. London: UCET.

WHITE, P. (1983) *Beyond Domination*. London: Routledge and Kegan Paul.

WHITE, P. (1987) 'Self-respect, self-esteem and the management of Educational Institutions: A Question of Values.' *Educational Management and Administration*, 15, 2.

Index

access 7, 22, 30, 31, 46, 51, 53, 63, 95
accountability 3, 20, 22, 34, 49, 57, 63, 80, 84, 92
accountancy 19, 92, 110
achievement 19, 20, 21, 25, 26
ACSET 71, 72, 78, 80
ACSTT 72
administration 7, 58, 83, 85, 99, 108
adult education 2, 33, 46, 51, 52, 96
advisers and inspectors 29, 48, 64, 81, 82, 106, 108, 110, 111
AHM 95
aims 15
anthropology 15, 16
appraisal 33, 70, 71, 74, 79, 80–2, 83, 103, 110
Arendt, H. 26, 126
Arnold, T. 39
assisted places 35
Audit Commission 74, 83, 93, 97

Bains Report 48, 98, 126
Belbin, R. M. 69, 126
Bell, A. 82, 106, 126
Blake, W. 29
Board of Education 90
Bonbon-Pädagogik 18–19
Booth, T. 127
budget 67, 74, 83, 86, 87, 88, 90, 91, 99, 100, 104

cascade model 24, 106

CATE 78
central government 1, 6, 13, 16, 29, 33, 36, 38, 45, 47, 49, 55, 57, 80, 85, 93, 99, 101, 110
chief executive 90, 106, 110
head as 4, 66, 85
choice of school 55, 56, 57
CIPFA 92
classroom, 25, 38, 50, 59, 70, 77, 78, 83, 105, 108
Clough, E. 127
Clough, P. 127
clusters 6, 52, 59
collegiality 6, 26, 32, 40, 61, 66, 81
communication 7, 13, 30, 32, 34, 47, 60, 62, 63, 64, 70, 77, 79, 84, 87, 107, 112
community 2, 3, 6, 7, 10, 12, 13, 18, 21, 32, 33, 41, 43, 45–65, 67, 68, 76, 77, 84, 95, 96, 99, 100, 108, 111
competition 7, 21, 23, 26, 36, 52
comprehensive schools 10, 45, 49, 50, 51, 91, 92, 94, 106
computers 32, 34, 59, 64
conditions of service 13, 33, 36, 66, 69, 80, 83, 103, 106, 112
confidence 19
conflict 11, 20, 38, 40
consensus 37
consortia 59, 60, 79
continuity 45, 50, 51, 52, 93, 98
cooperation 7, 18, 25, 26, 31, 34,

35, 36, 46, 49, 57, 59, 63, 67, 81, 104, 111
corporate management 7, 10, 32, 43, 46, 48, 54, 90, 94, 99
cost centres 16
cost-effectiveness 32, 34
culture 10, 19, 20, 21, 22, 29, 32, 33, 35, 48
  of organisation 12, 16, 19, 27, 31, 53, 61, 107, 110
curriculum
  continuity of **49–51**
  control of 6, 47, 85
  development of 9, 27, 30, 32, 33, 56, 71, 79
  formal 7, 53
  hidden **9–11**, 96, 104
  national 7, 22, 29, 33, 34, 36, 50, 61, 66, 78
  negotiated 10, 63
  school 7, 52, 76

De Bono 38–9
De Jouvenel, B. 20–1, 126
democracy 4, 11, 17, 19, 26, 27, 28, 30, 55, 81, 116
department/faculty 6, 39
Department of Education and Science 29, 36, 49, 61, 69, 77, 87, 90, 92, 126–7
Department of Employment 36, 49
Department of the Environment 36, 93, 98
Department of Trade and Industry 4, 36, 49, 63, 107
development education 31, 32, 33
distance learning 6, 76
Drucker, P. F. 37, 127

education officers 10, 27, 43, 48, 81, 86, 93, 99, 110, 111, 112
Education Support Grant 88
effective school management 8, 13, 17, 18, 20, 24, 37, 51
elementary education 45, 49, 89, 106
employment 4, 30, 45, 46, 51, 52, 63, 64, 80, 107, 111, 115, 118

energy conservation 32, 34, 87, 94, 97
environmental care 2, 27, 31, 32
EPA 95
equal opportunities 10, 36, 53, 55, 112ff.
Europe 20
  Council of Europe 33
  Czechoslovakia 61, 106
  European Communities 11, 66, 114
  France 106
  Germany 30
evaluation 21, 78, 81
examinations 19, 29, 52, 85
  BTEC 52
  control of 6, 36, 37
  CPVE 52
  fees 87, 91
  GCSE 26, 52, 106
  publication of results 35
  reform of 13, 30, 37

federal school 6
Fish Report 67, 127
Fisher, H. A. L. 35
force field analysis 40–3
formula funding 88
freedom 10, 16
further education 2, 9, 24, 51, 59, 66, 89, 92

General Teaching Council 13, 20, 80, 111, **117–25**
governors 3, 10, 20, 34, 37, 47–9, 52–3, 57, 59, 63, 66–7, 75, 80, 82, 84, 87, 89–90, 94, 99, 100, 104, 108, 111, 118
  training of 33, 61, 64, 68
grant-maintained schools 33, 52, 57
Great Debate 72
GRIST 72, 74
group learning 8, 12, 21, 23, 31, 40, 41, 77, 79, 82
grouping policy 24, 25, 43

Halsey, A. H. 99, 127
Handy, C. B. 17, 127
Hargreaves, A. 76, 127

heads 5, 7, 27, 39–40, 49, 60–1, 66–8, 70, 81, 83, 86–7, 91–2, 94–5, 97, 99–100, 104–8, 110
Headmasters' Association 90, 92, 95, 127
health service 46, 48, 53
Hegel, G. 11
Her Majesty's Inspectorate 13, 27, 29, 60, 106, 110, 112, 126–7
hierarchy 19, 30–1, 34, 39–40, 81
higher education 30, 51, 79, 110
  training institutions 71, 79
Hilsum, S. 83, 127
Hobbes, T. 26
home and family 10, 31, 46–7, 56, 84, 108, 111
Home Office Section 11
  funding 82, 88
housing 46, 48
Hoyle, E. 16, 127
Hughes, M. 4, 127

induction 67, 70–1
industry 4, 16, 29, 37, 51, 52, 92, 96, 106, 107, 114
information technology 7, 54, 64
initial training 10, 19, 25, 33, 62, 67, 70, 72, 78, 110
INSET 25, 33, 43, 67–8, 71–5, 78–80, 115
institutions 11–12, 15–18, 22, 30, 34, 50, 62, 76, 110
integration 53
international 30
involvement 12, 40, 46, 54, 57, 74
ISIS 36

James Report 71–2, 126
Jarratt Report 16
John, D. W. 60, 127
Jones, A. 127
Jones, N. 19, 77, 78, 127

Knight, B. 91

Labriola, A. 20
Lancaster, J. 82, 106, 127
LEA 11–13, 16, 20, 29, 47–8, 57, 68, 70–1, 74, 80, 82, 85, 88–94, 96–7, 99, 101
  Cambridgeshire 46, 96–8, 100
  Cheshire 97
  East Sussex 97
  Grampian 67
  ILEA 67, 95, 98
  Leicestershire 46, 96
  Lincolnshire 98
  Oxfordshire 97–8, 100
  Solihull 97, 100
  Somerset 97
  Surrey 97
LEA training grants 72, 74, 88
leadership 4, 5, 10, 54, 59–61, 66–7, 85, 112, 116
learning 2, 17, 21, 22–5, 27, 47, 65
  experience 3, 8, 10, 13, 32, 50, 72, 76, 84, 114
  lifelong 31–2, 50–1, 53, 80
  management of 38
  modular 72–3, 79, 84
  opportunities 8, 22, 25, 50, 76
  partnership in 24, 38
  process 8, 27, 60, 110
  programmes 31–2
  skills 8–9
legislation 11–12, 30, 32–4, 45, 47–8, 50, 52–4, 56–7, 65–6, 87, 89, 94, 103
local financial management 34, 37, 47, 52–3, 58–9, 61, 66–9, 74, 82, 83, 85–104
Locke, J. 26

Macchiavelli, N. 26
Mandela, W. 19
marketing 27
market forces 1, 3, 35–6, 52, 61
Marxism 11, 20
McIntyre, A 17
media 2, 35, 50, 64, 76–7, 79, 111
middle management 12, 66, 107–8, 111
Morris, H. 46

negotiation 38, 53, 77, 79, 83
Nixon, J. 127

open
 college 6, 59
 enrolment 7, 34, 51
 schooling 6, 59
 university 6, 59
organisation 5–7, 9, 12, 15,
 29–31, 33, 36, 38–41, 43, 46,
 54, 61, 64, 66–7, 71, 74, 78,
 81, 83, 94, 100, 104, 107–8,
 112

parents 10, 22, 29, 34–6, 38, 43,
 51, 54–7, 61–2, 65, 68, 70,
 80, 82, 84, 86, 96–7, 100, 111
participation 1, 10, 31
partnership 35, 38, 47, 52, 54, 57,
 59, 63, 82, 92, 112
pastoral care 39, 49, 70, 108
perestroïka 61
philosophy 15–16, 22
physical environment 9, 58, 64,
 85, 91
plant 30, 32, 58, 116
Plowden Report 50
police 34, 48, 53
politics 1, 3, 10–11, 16, 22–3, 27,
 29–30, 35–7, 39–41, 46–7,
 48, 51, 74, 86, 93, 98–9, 104
polytechnics 112
Potts, P. 127
power 2, 3, 21–2, 26, 30–1, 40–1,
 81, 103
 sharing 40, 47, 64
primary education 2, 45, 50, 51,
 89, 103
private sector 35, 89
privilege 30, 45, 55
probation of teachers 70
profession 3, 5, 7, 11, 13, 20, 27,
 29, 36, 38, 46, 61, 64, 66, 75,
 81, 83, 108, 111, 117
professional development 13, 31,
 34, 37, 41, 52, 62–3, 68–9,
 71, 74, 111
professional tutor 67, 70–1, 108
progression 38
psychology 8, 15–16, 21, 24–5,
 69, 78, 108, 110–12

public relations 59

Redcliffe-Maud Report 47, 89,
 127
regional development 32, 46,
 79–80, 112, 116
research 16, 36, 43
resources
 allocation of 24, 43, 83, 93, 95
 management of 4–5, 8, 12, 21,
 32, 34, 41, 64, 67–8, 77, 85ff.
 of community 2, 50, 53–4, 79
 use of 9, 17, 32
responsibility 19–20, 40, 51, 59,
 61, 64, 66–7, 75–6, 86, 104,
 107–8, 111, 114
review 70, 79, **80–2**
rights 22, 31–3
Romme, C. 33
rural education 46, 92
Russell, B. 26, 127

Sayer, J. 14, 67, 77–8, 127
Schools Council 6
secondary schools 2, 9, 24, 29,
 45–7, 50–1, 66, 83, 89–90,
 94, 97, 103
 Holyrood, Chard 91
self-management 12, 112
self-esteem 19, 27
senior management team 5, 10,
 39–40, 63, 105, 110
SHA 82, 90
sharing 2–3, 12, 14, 19–20, 29,
 31, 38, 51, 54, 68, 79, 110
Shaw, B. 40
skills 8–9, 12–13, 18, 22, 30–1,
 100
social
 background 33, 79
 change and reform 10, 50, 84,
 92, 104
 reconstruction 3, 6, 46, 54
 services 46
society 5, 13–15, 17–18, 20,
 22–3, 26–8, 30, 32, 39, 53, 83
sociology 15–16
South Africa 16
Soweto 16

special educational needs   24, 33,
    51, 53, 76, 88, 94
sports   46
staff   27, 39, 100, 104, 108
    college   116
stuffing 49, 52, 57, 74, 81, **82–4**,
    87, 95
staff room   67, **75–6**, 106
statutory services   48, 65
Strong, C.   83, 127

Taylor Report   48, 52, 89, 99
teachers   1, 13, 27, 29, 37–8, 62,
    66–84, 85
teachers' centres   64
teamwork   17, 19–21, 23, 25,
    31–2, 34, 54, 57, 61, 63–4,
    77, 81, 110
technicians   58, 78
timetable   33, 78, 83, 85
training
    heads   24, 107
    management   9, 18, 38, 61, 64,
        105–7, 110, **115–17**
    non-teachers   68

Training Agency   49, 93
tutor   31–2, 51, 62–3, 65, 77, 82,
    108
TVEI   52, 58

UCET   80
universities   16, 19, 29, 51, 85
UNO   33
urban   46, 92
Urban Aid   33, 88

values   13, **15–28**, 54, 86, 104–5
virement   7, 63, 86, 91, 93–4, 100
vision   13, 62, 76
voluntary   46–7, 65, 83

Warnock Report   57, 95
Weaver Report   117
welfare   46
White, P.   19, 128
women in teaching   10, 68, 108,
    112–15

youth service   2, 46, 51, 59, 96
YTS   52